COUNT
YOUR
Blessings

A BOOK OF
TESTIMONIES

COUNT YOUR

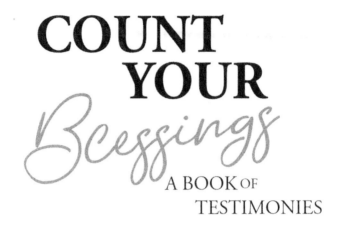

Blessings

A BOOK OF
TESTIMONIES

VEE NATHAN

POLYMER
PRESS

LONDON

Count Your Blessings: A Book of Testimonies
Text copyright © 2020 by Devalletta Nathan
Pen name: Vee Nathan

Polymer Press
ISBN: 978-1-9162962-0-6

First edition published in London, United Kingdom in 2020 by Polymer Press a trading name of Devalletta Nathan.
First printed in the United Kingdom in 2020.

Cover design by COLONFILM | Flor Figueroa.

A copy of this book can be found in the British Library.

www.veenathan.com

Acknowledgements

··•●•··

I would like to thank my sister Val and my Pastor's wife Pearl for their encouragement in taking time to proofread and provide valuable feedback on the contents of this book.

I'd also like to thank my niece (and goddaughter) Samantha for her support and encouragement in editing it. And, last but by no means least, my daughter Nadya for her patience and determination to see this work complete. For believing in and encouraging me, for her constant reminders to keep on going on to the end, and for all her unstinting effort in researching all the many and various details that has led to the cover design and publishing of this book. I love and appreciate you all.

Contents

Introduction

·· ● ·· ●

This book is a record of moments in my life when God revealed himself to me in various ways. It is primarily a recalling of specific moments or incidents that serve to highlight my relationship with him. Of necessity, others will be mentioned in the process, some by name, some not. They are simply illustrations of what was going on in my life at the time. Some of these examples also helped me to focus on my relationship with God the Father and allowed me to see the work of the Holy Spirit in my life all brought about by the saving grace of my Lord and Saviour Jesus Christ. It is not my life story, just snippets God has asked me to record for the glory and honour of His Holy Name.

It is about how God aided and enabled me to cope in difficult, challenging and sometimes overwhelming situations. As well as being about asking and receiving, listening and hearing, pain and healing, tears and laughter, war and peace, death and life and so much more from the life of an ordinary woman made extraordinary by God.

To make sense of it all, I will provide some background information, which may cast individuals in a negative image. This is not my intention and is not a criticism of them.

The Question That Started It All

···•◕•···

After 18 years of what I thought was a happy marriage, I asked my husband one night if he loved me. I don't know why I asked such a question; I certainly had not planned to or had any doubts about the answer I would receive. You can imagine my shock and distress then when after a long silence he informed me that he "couldn't say...was not sure!" My world spiralled out of control at that moment and I felt sick. I remember questioning myself, asking, "why did you ask that question, what possessed you to ask such a question?". Even now I have no idea. But the truth was out and had to be dealt with. It was tough, we talked and talked, and I thought we had begun to find our footing again. We did not seek counselling immediately but had agreed we would and life went on as usual, or so it would appear to observers. To me, something fundamental had changed and I knew that whatever the outcome following counselling, it would never be the same again because I would never be the same again. A year later, shortly after our nineteenth anniversary, he informed me he was leaving, and left a few weeks later. He

3

made his decision even though we did not receive marriage counselling.

Sometime in 2001, and a little over 2 years after my husband and I had separated, I was going through a particularly rough patch emotionally. I had gone to bed feeling low and, foolishly, had chosen to wallow in self-pity when I should have risen in praise. The result was a natural plummeting to some place I hope never to return to again. God, my loving Father rescued me in the most memorable way. In a nutshell, He told me to count my blessings. I obeyed and began to consider all the good things in my life. Then He told me I should begin with my earliest memories, so I went back in time as far as I could. Having done so, I was soon lost in this exercise and had arrived at about age 15 when He told me to write my testimony. I got up and began to write with zeal. Needless to say my spirit was restored as I began to realise just how much God had done for me and how truly blessed I was to be known by Him. There have been long periods of time when I have written nothing, not because I had nothing to write, but because I am a working concern in the Father's hand when it comes to procrastination –

but I am on the road to victory! God won this one, of course, and here is the result.

Oh, by the way, do you remember this chorus of a song? It was one of my Sunday School favourites.

Count your blessings, name them one by one
Count your blessings, see what God has done
Count your blessings, name them one by one
And it will surprise you what the Lord has done.

Well, I wasn't surprised by how much He had done, just at how much I had forgotten. The memory of it all acted like a tonic and my flagging spirit was revived, as was my thankfulness and appreciation for all I had received at His hand.

Memories

From as far back as I can remember God was there, unacknowledged, but present. My first memory is of my grandfather's funeral. I was two years old and I remember being held by my sister, Ann, who carried me from the pew where we sat, to the right of the aisle and about a quarter of the way down from the back of the church, to the front of the church to join the procession of family and friends walking around the coffin to take a last look at the deceased 'Barda-K' as he was called (spelt phonetically); his name was Caleb Ellis. I don't believe she intended that I see him lying in his coffin because I remember being held close and looking over her shoulder at the people behind her as she moved forward to see grandfather for the last time. I must have turned in her arms because I saw his face. Many years later when I looked at the face of my father for the last time, this memory came flooding back like an action replay. Whatever the case, my mother approached very angry that I had seen his face, it's not healthy for a young child I suppose, and shoved my sister and me in the direction of the door. I remember being amongst many people in my sisters' arms outside the church waiting. Though I must have met my grandfather many times, the only memory I have is of him in his coffin with family and friends gathered to sing songs of thanksgiving to God for his life.

The second memory that stands out in my mind is of an incident involving a black car. I was about two and a half years old; at least, that's what my mother told me when I recounted this event to her years later. She was very surprised that I remembered either of these events. My sister, Ann, had taken me to fetch water from the standpipe not far from home, and situated within sight of the main road. When our bucket was nearly full, she saw the car approaching. She turned the tap off, grabbed the bucket and me, and ran for cover in the nearby bushes. I remember the urgency of her actions instilled fear in me and I looked for the cause. She was afraid and peered intensely through the bushes toward the car slowing to a stop, just below the standpipe, which was set on an incline on the side of the road. Two men in dark suits got out and looked at the tap that was still dripping, to the left and the right of the tap, at the bushes, up and down the road, and then returned to their car and drove off. Meanwhile, I was held un-comfortably tight with a hand over my mouth, my sister hardly breathed, and though I did not hear it, I'm sure she was praying. When the men drove off she scooped me up into her arms, grabbed the bucket and hurried home. I am told that around this time there had been many reports of children being kidnapped, young girls in particular. My mother is amazed that I remember these events young as I was. So am I.

* * *

My father left Jamaica in 1958 when I was just months old, and my mother joined him in 1962 leaving us in the care of our aunt and uncle. I came to England in 1963 with my 3 brothers and sister to join my parents. We had a new sister waiting to meet us. I was not too pleased as I had been the baby of the family with all its benefits up until then. I demanded to know where she came from. Mum said she'd asked God for a baby and the angel brought her. I was 5½ years old and believed every word.

We went to the local Methodist Church and Sunday school every week without fail. We attended that church, as it was conveniently close, within walking distance. We were the best-dressed and best-behaved children there. Going to church was a serious matter, one not to be taken lightly. Idle chatter or poor behaviour got you a look from mum that quashed any thoughts of rebellion. By word and actions we were taught that God was to be respected, honoured, worshipped, praised; that He should be given our best at all times, that Sunday was His day and our opportunity to say thank you.

Sunday was marked as a special day, not just because of the dressing up, or going to church, or the delicious meals mum prepared. On Sundays there was no loud boisterous play, no visiting (that took place on Saturday), no popular or secular music from the gramophone or radio. Sunday was sacred music time – Skeeta Davis, Jim Reeves and the like. It was a quiet, contemplative, family day disturbed only by our laughter, and we laughed a lot.

My father knew of God but did not submit to His Lordship until later in life. My mother on the other hand, was God-fearing and a committed Christian. By the time I was six years old I was aware of God's existence. I knew that He protected us, heard and answered our prayers, that He desired our best at all times and that one of seven days belonged to Him; I strove to do my best.

Mum often punctuate her sentences with phrases like "if it weren't for God" and "God willing", so I came to know that He was actively involved in our day-to-day living and should be included in our decision making. I remember her speaking of the foolishness of people who believed they could live their lives without God and hope to achieve anything worth keeping without His help.

In our home, my father laid down the law with regards to behaviour and expectations, with my mum in agreement. They always spoke from the same sheet and supported and re-enforced each other's discipline, but mum was the chief disciplinarian where rules/boundaries were flouted. This was probably because she was always there on site, while my dad worked long hours to support his family. We called her the "sheriff", though not to her face until we were grown. She was firm and we were all in awe of her.

I rarely made the same mistake twice, a lesson learnt once was a lesson learnt for life. On some occasions when discipline was required, she would sometimes have tears in her eyes. I used to think if disciplining us upset her so much, why do it? More than once I can remember her making reference to "sparing the rod and spoiling the child". It seems that would have been an unthinkable crime, so we were not spoilt. As a mother now, I realise that we must have been a handful, all 8 of us. I now know what a difficult but necessary part of parenting discipline is, and quite possibly as painful for the parent, as it is for the child.

When I look at the problems in society today, much due to a lack of discipline, I thank God for my parents and the value they placed on our lives, and for the values they instilled in us from an early age. Mum said "a child had to be shaped and moulded when young, otherwise, like a tree, if you tried to bend it when old, it would break". In other words, it would be too late and the damage done!

When I was eleven years old, we moved home and our family attended the local Elim Pentecostal Church. This was more to my mother's liking and we settled there. My father, I called him Papa, attended on special occasions only. Our family took up almost a whole row of seats. I loved the songs, enjoyed singing and I sometimes enjoyed the word or teaching, which meant I was able to focus on what was being said. Oftentimes though, I would allow my attention to wander and struggle to stay awake. I think it was more concern for Mum's disapproval than God's judgement that kept my eyes open; I always looked forward to and enjoyed Sunday school though.

As I grew into my mid teen years, the Sunday morning service became more of a ritual for me. I went through the motions because I knew it was the right thing to do, but I yearned for change, though I did not know what form this should take. By this time I'd heard hundreds of sermons and bible lessons, but they held my interest for a few minutes only – I'd heard it all before and I wanted something new. How many different ways could you tell someone that God loved and had died for them? I knew that, so what! What was I to do about it?

It wasn't until I was 17 yrs old that I actually heard God speak to me. My pastor was preaching on Gods' love, again, when suddenly he seemed to be speaking to me. I looked at him, he appeared to be looking at me, but it was God who spoke and my heart jumped in fright. Even when he appeared to look away, I still felt God's eyes on me. I could not escape His gaze. I felt exposed, and when He said, "come", I felt I had no choice. I raised my hand (half mast) in acknowledgement of His call, but went no further. I rationalised that I had imagined it all (I have a vivid imagination). Why would God want me and what sin had I committed? With parents like mine you were fearful of being detected with a bad thought. Sin to me meant some great misdeed like lying, stealing or immorality. They were some of the things my parents had forbidden; therefore, I was not a sinner – not really.

Life went on as usual but I felt more and more guilty; each sermon seemed to speak directly to me. Twice more I raised my hand during the altar call so God would see I had acknowledged his call, and then rapidly tried to forget it all. I thought, and knew, my life would change and I liked it the way it was. Also try as I would, I could not identify anything I recognised as sin in my life so what was I to be saved from? I was OK. But a feeling of dread steadily crept up on me and I knew I'd been lying to myself. I had to make a decision for God and stand by it but was suddenly assailed by doubts. What was real or true? Was I having an emotional experience? I did not know what to believe and was afraid I'd be deceived. Going to bed that night I prayed and asked God to speak to me, to make it clear what He wanted of me.

As it turned out, and you've probably guessed, it was not what He wanted from me, but more what He had to give me.

The Vision

··•●•··

That night my sleep was disturbed and I woke up aware that I was not alone. I was not afraid; the uppermost emotion I experienced was calm even though my heart was pounding. Eyes still closed, I tried to get a sense of who was there and where they were without success but felt that eyes were focussed on me. Finally, I opened my eyes. My room was pitch black, unnaturally dark for a moment. There appeared in the centre of the room, a large sword, which reminded me of the Wilkinson's Sword razor advert of the 70s, 'Name of the World's Finest Blade'. As soon as I saw the sword, a voice spoke to me and instructed me to "lie down". It seemed to come from everywhere, not from any particular point in the room; I knew the voice, but didn't know how.

As I was asked to lie down, I became aware that the sword actually represented a bed, so I very naturally refused, believing I would be killed. Again, the voice gently and encouragingly commanded me to "lie down", but this time I explained that the sword was so sharp that if I obeyed, I'd be cut in two! Its blade was gleaming, reflecting some invisible light. I reached forward, extended my right hand, and with my thumb tested the blade, it was razor sharp. I could not understand why He, by this time I knew it was God, wanted me to do something that was potentially dangerous and life threatening. I sensed that He drew near to me and He said, "lie down, try me and prove me. With me you are safe". At these words a white lace pillow appeared at the hilt of the sword and three gleaming white steps to the side for me to climb onto the sword-bed. Heart pounding, I began to climb the steps all the while thinking 'He said I would be safe'. As I got to the top of the steps, I placed both hands and my right knee onto the bed and prepared to lie down. Bracing myself, eyes shut tight, I lay down and cringed as I expected to feel the sharp blade cut through me. Instead, I felt myself sinking into a wonderful, cotton wool softness going down several feet it seemed before rising slowly upward into a piercing, glowing, white light full of warmth, and I heard myself cry, "Oh yes, you're right. With you I am safe!" I was thrilled, filled with joy and wonder. I had expected to die, but instead, I was alive.

Suddenly the light, the sword, everything disappeared and I was sitting up in bed. I looked around my room and could just about see the dark outline of my bed, wardrobe, dressing table and the faint glow of grey moonlight around the edges of the curtains of the French window. At first I thought, "was that a dream?" but I knew it wasn't as I was already awake. I remember feeling that I was not alone in my room. It was God – I recognised His voice. I pinched myself, literally, touched the bed, got up and put the light on. I looked around, and was convinced it wasn't a dream. I put the light out, went back to bed, and said aloud "Yes Lord, I will serve you".

It was at that point that I knew without a doubt that God loved me and all He wanted was to save me. I'd asked Him to make it clear what he wanted from me, and He did. He wanted me to trust Him, to give my life to Him, and in return, He gave it right back...debt free. I'd had a sense of finality about the whole thing, like it was one of those now or never situations. I knew this opportunity would not be repeated. If I rejected Him when He brought his invitation personally, what hope would there be for me? He loved me so much that He came to my bedroom to tell me and put all my fears to rest. This time I responded with my whole heart.

I felt shame at thinking I was without sin as God revealed my sins to me. I asked and He forgave me and replaced my tears with joy. I could not return to sleep that night; I was so excited I just lay there in the dark soaking up Gods' love like a sponge and watching the dawn appear. Finally, it was morning and I woke my mother to tell her my news, the whole vision and my response. She was so happy. I was the first of Gods answer to her many prayers for the salvation of her children. I was 18 years old.

I attended baptism classes and was baptised shortly after. That was an amazing experience in itself. I fully appreciated the doctrine of death to the old self and rising in the newness of life in the Spirit. I felt brand new and as light as a feather, waterlogged as I was, and with not a care in the world. He certainly took all my guilt, shame and burdens away. Sometime after this I attended a rally at the Royal Albert Hall where I received baptism in the Holy Spirit and experienced speaking in tongues.

Now, 43 years later I have a catalogue of testimonies to Gods' love and provision. Over and over again, at different times and in different situations, I have tried Him, and each time, He has kept His promise to me and kept me safe.

Salvation for those I loved the most

··•●•··

Following my encounter with God in my bedroom, I rang my Pastor and arranged to see him. At the interview I told him of my experience and resulting decision to accept Christ as my Lord and Saviour and to be baptised. I waited with excitement for Sunday when I would tell the whole church of my decision to follow Jesus. I felt ten feet tall and wanted the world to know. I had not told the rest of my family yet, so on my way home from the interview with my Pastor, I decided to tell them.

I don't remember why I did not have or did not use my front door key. I was probably too excited at the prospect of telling my family. Anyway, I rang the doorbell and my eldest brother opened up for me – I was so pleased it turned out to be him. It seemed right and proper that the eldest should be the first to know. Also, I looked up to him, and felt sure he would be pleased for me. WRONG! When I blurted out excitedly that I had become a Christian, he looked at me, puzzled and sad all at once, and frowning at me he said, "Vee, you're only eighteen and you've thrown your life away." If disappointment could kill, I would have died right there. I had been so sure he would be happy for me that I felt the tears stinging the back of my eyes, my throat was tight with emotion. I felt *so* hurt by his remark, and did not know how to begin to explain that I had actually just found my life. How do you explain the joy you feel bubbling continually inside? How do you explain that a flower is no longer just a flower, but the most fantastic and beautiful example of the creative power and beauty of a loving Father? How do you explain that green grass is greener, blue sky is bluer than ever before, and that with Christ within, I was experiencing real life for the first time, and what I had before was just a shadow in comparison! I could not find the words to explain all this and the lump in my throat was threatening to overwhelm me, so I went straight to my bedroom and closed the door, turning the key in the lock as I did so. I knelt by my bed and cried out to God for my brother, for my whole family. I asked God to save them, to let them know the joy and life I was experiencing. I told Him how much I loved them and how much it hurt to think of them suffering eternally. When I could not find the words to express how I felt I just sobbed, groaned and cried, "Please...please...".

Some time during that prayer I found myself looking up at a very high building whose top seemed to disappear in the clouds. I entered the building but found I had actually entered a large lift and the door closed as it began its' journey upward. I was aware that the lift was full, that there was a large group of passengers standing behind me as I stood facing the door. I could hear their voices but had not been able to see them. I turn my head, first to the right, then to the left, looking behind me, and there were all my brothers and sisters, my whole family! I did not see and recognise individual faces, it was more like I'd spiritually discerned them whilst I was standing in the forefront of the crowded lift. I saw others in the background but did not know who they were. As I looked, the lift began its' journey upward and became filled with light that became brighter and whiter the higher up we went, until there was only light. I became aware that I was still on my knees by my bed. My tears dried as I realised God had shown me the answer to my prayer. I was at peace and felt calm and confident. The hurt and pain was gone. I knew I could trust God. I could not stop smiling and thanking Him, I must have smiled for days because people I did not know were smiling and greeting me. I wondered where I had met them.

Today all my family (7 brothers and sisters) are saved and serving God in various ministries. Over recent years we have celebrated Christmases together, my mum (my father is with the Lord), brothers and sisters and their families. We repeated this family gathering once or twice during the year also. One such occasion was my eldest brother's 50th birthday. While we were all in the garden enjoying a lovely BBQ, I looked amongst all the invited guests that were my family. I saw how close we still were and suddenly realised that with my youngest brother's recent conversion, my whole family that I had prayed for were now saved, just as I had asked God and He had promised. I felt the tears prickling the back of my eyes again as my throat tightened. I remembered the vision in my bedroom. Twenty-five years later, that promise was fulfilled. God is awesome! None of His words return empty. None of His promises unfulfilled. He is faithful, trustworthy, and dependable. I felt blessed that this mighty God cared enough for me to give me a promise, and allow me to live to see it fulfilled. Silently I praised His name and gave thanks.

Life and Death

·· • ● • ··

My impression of my father is that he was a quiet man who enjoyed a good joke, was a great storyteller but had no time for idle chatter. As I said before, he laid down the law and my mother enforced it. I did not misinterpret his quietness for weakness, lack of interest or anything like that; I looked up to him and had a proper regard for his rules and desire to see us do well. I wanted to do well to please him. I was proud of him. As a child, on the few occasions when I walked down the street with him, just the two of us, I would walk tall and look closely at the faces of everyone walking toward us, wondering if they could see just how great my dad was. Of course, they couldn't – children have such vivid imaginations.

My father became a Christian three years before he went to be with the Lord. His passing was a terrible blow to us all. He was a fairly young man in his 50s. It was during one of the coldest winters on record, the winter of '78/79 and the ground was frozen solid so there was a developing crisis in the mortuaries as funerals could not take place. It was about four weeks before I had the opportunity to finally say goodbye to my dad. This was due to the severe weather conditions that had delayed the funeral ceremony. I felt my pain and mourning was at once extended and suspended! I knew I had lost my father but because there was no funeral, I almost believed he was still around, just away somewhere. The array of family and friends that visited to give their condolences and encouragements, as was customary, seemed to go on forever, lending a sense of the unreal to the whole situation. As their conversations focused on memories of my dad and his exploits, there was lots of laughter just like when he was alive, so it was a strange period of mourning. I would not have been surprised if he'd just walked through the door. So, my dad was very much alive in our day-to-day chatter and I longed to see him just one more time.

Finally, his funeral loomed large and the day before his body was laid to rest, he was brought home and laid out in a beautiful casket set up in the front room as tradition demanded. Arriving home from work that Friday evening, I was excited to see him. He had 'fallen asleep' 10 days after my 21st birthday and I was still struggling with the knowledge that he was actually gone. I don't know what I expected but it was certainly not what I saw. He looked great. Handsome and smart in his favourite suit surrounded by a mass of white studded satin, and it seemed like he was asleep. I tried to hold his hand one last time but it was cold and rigid in its white glove. I didn't quite expect that, having never been this close to 'death' before. I wanted to talk to him and did, though only God knows all that I said. Just chit-chat I suppose. I touched his chest and face – it was hard and cold. How strange, I thought, that he should appear to be sleeping. When I accepted that he could not hear me, I spoke to God instead. I remember the conversation, it went something like this, "He's not here is he? He's with you. You've taken your breath back haven't you?" I continued to look at the body lying there. Seeing how beautifully it had been crafted; every detail was perfect. I saw my father as a work of art and thought "isn't God great? Just look at what He's done". Very softly His Spirit spoke to mine and said, "this is how I created man, this is what he was before I breathed my Spirit into him and he became a living soul". I remember thinking, "wow…what power".

Mentally, I reversed the process and imagined my father breathing and speaking again, then looked at the empty shell that had been the housing for the soul and spirit that had been my father and was awed at the greatness of God. I stood there for ages marvelling at what God could do, and had done, and smiling because I knew where my father was. That was the moment I fully understood the creation story; that I completely understood that without God, we are nothing. It was also at that moment that I understood the warning that we should not fear the one that could destroy the body or flesh, but the one who could destroy the soul. Why? Because the body is no more than a beautiful but empty shell without the breath of God; of no value whatsoever in eternity! In fact, it has no place in eternity. We are told that we shall be changed and the perishable (flesh) shall become the imperishable (spirit). Hence the saying, "if your eye or hand offends, gouge it out or cut it off". We don't need them where we're going, but they can prove a hindrance to our getting there if they continually cause offence. But for as long as we have the breath of God, our bodies are the housing for the soul and spirit; those parts of ourselves that continue, that are imperishable and that commune with God, responds to his love and is truly alive.

At that moment, the fear of finally admitting that he was gone, and the terrible pain of grief that I had expected to feel and had been afraid of, failed to materialise. Death, for me, had definitely lost its sting. It was not the horror I had thought it to be, as the world believed and portrayed it, a negative and fearful thing; it was as Jesus said, a "falling asleep", and in that knowledge, a thing of great beauty. Of course, I realise this is a matter of opinion depending on what you believe, and where you stand in relation to Christ Jesus. This realisation did not mean that my grieving was over, because I missed my dad and could not hear an ABBA hit on the radio without bursting into tears many months after – my boss got the worst of it as he could not seem to work without the radio – they were my dad's favourite band. No, I had not ceased to mourn; it was just that my grief was tempered with joy.

Marriage

·· • ● •· ··

I left school at 16 years of age and attended a College of Further Education. This came about when I failed to control my very real but quietly rebellious streak. I'm not proud of it, but have to smile at the memory. You see, I thought I was grown and did not appreciate being told what I must do or where I should go with regards to further education, and being offered (with hindsight I now realise) wise counsel. So, I made all the arrangements myself, informed the school head that I was leaving, arranged and attended interviews at colleges. When the first day of term came and I presented myself dressed in black trousers and a yellow tank top ready to start the new academic year, Mum wanted to know why I was not in uniform. I responded casually while quaking in my shoes that we were allowed to wear trousers in sixth form, but that I had, in fact, left school and was on my way to college, and sauntered out of the room. I can still hear her words ringing in my ears, "We'll discuss this when you get home", having first called upon God "to see her trial". I arrived home to an inquisition from Mum, Dad and several older brothers and sister. I answered their questions with a nonchalance I was far from feeling. There was no going back, of course, which is what I'd intended. They said their piece; I listened politely and then went my way thinking "Yeah".

Until I started college, the only men in my life were my father, uncles, brothers, cousins and a few of my brothers' friends that my parents approved of. This meant that they were polite, well-mannered, respectful and ambitious young men, otherwise they would not have been allowed to cross the threshold, or so it seemed to me. I'm sure the truth was not very different. At 16 years of age I was considered too young to have a boyfriend, though most of my friends had one. Nothing was said directly, it was an unspoken understanding. The emphasis was on education. It had never really bothered me that I could not have a boyfriend, but when I started college a whole new world opened up and I chaffed against it a little, but not for long. I had led a sheltered life, had attended an all girls' school of my quietly rebellious and manipulative choosing (how could I ever have thought I did not need saving?). Some say that all girls' schools are the worst, and with hindsight, mine was probably up

there with the best of them, but it had somehow managed to bypass me. Most of my
friends labelled me as 'innocent'. I think this
was because I would not go against what I'd
been taught, even though my parents would
not have known any different.

I had many proposals to enter into relationships at college and refused them all, initially
because I knew my parents would not approve,
and as time went on, because I could not either. It was strange, but the more exposed I
was to young men, the more repulsed I was by
their seeming shallowness. I did not know
then that they matured at a *much* slower rate
than girls. I'm sure I wasn't taught that at
school, or maybe I missed it, being too busy by
sneakily reading Mills & Boons novels under
my textbooks. I began to think there was much
in my mother's attitude where they were concerned. They needed more time to grow up. I
hope I'm not offending anyone in recalling
this. Remember, I was very young myself. It
seemed there was some kind of competition
amongst them; the winner would be the one
who'd had the most girlfriends. I was determined not to be among those. The boys talked
about parties, fast cars, girls and clothes so
you quickly lost them if you talked about any-

thing else or horror of horrors, tried to discuss the subject we were all studying.

My friends thought I was crazy not to accept any of the proposed pairings, especially as the relationship could be kept within the confines of the college, but dishonesty (says the practicing rebel) did not come easy to me. I was taught to speak the truth and could do nothing else. When boys pressed me to 'go out' with them, I would eventually tell them to get permission from my parents if they were serious. This quickly put an end to the pestering, as I knew it would. It rapidly became my first line of defence against unwanted attention.

When I became a Christian, I looked about me for Christian young men but there was then, as there seems to be now, a dearth of them. I wasn't bothered much. Life was good and full of the things that interested me, family, friends, theatre, art, concerts, meals uptown (central London), books, books, and more books, I was content.

My dream was no different to that of any other young woman; marriage, home, children and a long happy life. A career was in there somewhere and I was working toward one, but it was not a need for me, more an expectation from others and it made sense from a practical point of view. I had no doubt it would happen one day. One day I would begin, like my older sister, to fill my 'bottom drawer' (buy stuff for my future home).

Strict as my parents were, family life was a very happy one, and I hoped to replicate it one day. I thought I'd have 5 children, until I gave birth and rapidly revised my plans. By now I was close to my twentieth birthday, getting on with my studies and enjoying life. Every so often I'd think about the future, look at the young men, or lack of them, in church, and then get on with the business of living. I really wasn't bothered because I was young, so I was quite surprised when my mother broached the subject. I suppose she was a little worried because I seemed to not show any of the natural interest in the opposite sex that a teenager (a few months short of my twentieth birthday) should. My response was that although I'd hoped to meet someone one day, at the moment I was not interested.

In the final year of my 3-year Sandwich Course in Dental Technology at South London College, and shortly before my 21st birthday, mum had another chat with me on one of my infrequent weekend visits home. My response was basically the same; I was not interested and had no time for a relationship. At that time I was living in Crowborough, East Sussex, and working in a dental laboratory in Tunbridge Wells, a short walk from the train station. I had decided not to return to college full-time for the final year of my course, but to complete it on a day release basis, which was one of the many options for this course. I thought no more of our conversation and concentrated on my final exams that were looming large – I was in revision mode. I spread my books over my bed in preparation and knelt by my dressing table to pray for God's support during this period.

To my surprise I heard myself say "oh God" and that was it. A floodgate burst open, I know not from where...I was overwhelmed with emotion and sobbed and sobbed. I could not understand where this had suddenly come from, and I could not stop. I tried to pray about my exams but found myself talking to God about myself, about the person I was and the values I had. About my desire to marry and have children, the husband I desired and the lack of Christian young men with such values and ambitions. I ended by reminding God that He knew me better than I knew myself and asking Him to look amongst His children for a young man He knew would make me a good husband. I gave some specifications of physical and spiritual attributes but left the final tweaking and decision to God. I asked Him to present this person to me when He thought I was ready for marriage and finally I asked that I recognise this person when we met, as I had no interest in moving from one boyfriend to another. All the while I was pouring my heart out to God, I felt I was somehow suspended in the air looking down on myself. I was amazed at what was happening but realised that every word spoken was heartfelt.

When I finished praying, I felt calm. I was totally confident that although it wasn't planned, it was right and it was now in God's hands so I had nothing to worry about. I washed my face, put my books away and went to bed still amazed at what had taken place, but sure in the knowledge it was of God.

Three weeks later my father died and a relationship was the last thing on my mind. Two months later I met my husband and as I saw him for the first time I recognised him as the one I had described to God, and even as recognition came, the Holy Spirit spoke to me and said, "here he is". I was dumbfounded! He had just graduated from Bible School and was appointed as the Assistant Pastor and Youth Leader at my home church. We had never had an Assistant Pastor in the ten years I had attended there. From here on until the end of morning worship, I was not aware of taking part in the meeting. I was too busy having a private conversation with God that went something like this.

God: Here he is.
Me: Yes, I see that, thank you. He looks like my description on the outside but what about inside Lord, what is he like inside?

At this point looking up at my husband-to-be standing beside my Pastor on the pulpit, I had a vision of his chest opening and inside it was filled with light and I saw the words love, kindness, patience, etc. I was shown the fruits of the Spirit and I was satisfied and said "oh yes, thank you". It then occurred to me that this had all taken place very quickly.

Me: But this is so soon, I didn't expect you to answer so soon, I'm only twenty-one – I'm too young!

God: But you said when I thought you were ready for marriage, I should send him, so here he is.

Me: I thought maybe when I was twenty-five

God: You said when I thought you were ready; you left the final decision to me

Me: Yes, you're right. Thank you...but God, he is a Pastor, I never said anything about a Pastor. I can't marry a Pastor. I'm the wrong kind of wife for a Pastor.

God: I know you best; I know what you can do. This is the one I've chosen for you.

Me: OK Lord, I trust you.

I sat there between my mother and sister, and went through the motions, all the while my thoughts were elsewhere as I tried to keep that young man in view. I first pondered on the speed with which God had answered my prayer and then at how clear and specific the answer was, leaving no room for doubt. I marvelled at the rolling conversation I'd had with Him just as though He were sitting or standing beside me in physical form. I began to understand His promise more fully, "Try me and prove me, with me you are safe". After some time of trying and failing to visualise myself as a Pastor's wife, I began to see the wisdom of being very specific in prayer when requesting anything of God. Words are powerful and should be used with care. I did not request a Pastor, but I did ask God to do what He knew was best for me and so He did, filling in the blank spaces left by me. All things considered, it was an awe inspiring moment that told me clearly that God loved me, was interested in all aspects of my life, and was literally only a prayer away.

At the end of the meeting, my husband-to-be stood at the exit with my Pastor, greeting members of the congregation as they left. As my mother approached my Pastor introduced her to him and they shook hands, followed by my sister and myself. He stumbled over my unusual name and smiled as he moved on to the next person. I returned the smile laughing inwardly as I considered how strange it was to be shaking the hand of my husband to be when he had no idea I was to be his wife! On the way home my family teased me quite a bit, saying what a nice young man our new Pastor seemed to be, just right for me. I laughed out loud sharing the moment with them while silently thinking "won't they be surprised in a few months time". He asked me out five weeks later, having first approached my Pastor and mother. We were married nine months after. God knows the deepest desires of our hearts and honours them as we seek to do His will. He should be Number One in our lives at all times.

Sad to say, but after 19 years together, my husband felt that he could not remain in the marriage and asked for a divorce having first informed me of the grounds on which I could obtain one. I will not go into details except to say that he refused wise counsel from Christian friends, including both our mothers and Pastor, in order to pursue his own goals. We were all devastated. It took me some time to grasp just how far he had removed himself from God. I forgave him but felt I could not divorce him, at the drop of a hat it seemed, without giving him time to realise what he had done and what it would mean, for our children especially. So I prayed and fasted and waited. In time God showed me clearly that there was no going back and I had to move forward with my life. I still loved my husband and found moving on difficult so one day I said to God, "you put this love in my heart for him, and now you're telling me this marriage is definitely over, so you had better take this love away again so I can close that door". I don't know exactly when it happened, but not long after that painful prayer I knew the door had been closed and my heart set free. It is impossible to tell you all God has done for me, or how much I love him, but if you continue reading you will get some idea.

After 3 years, my estranged husband returned to Trinidad in the Caribbean. He filed for divorce, and I signed the papers after 5 years. He has since remarried.

Over the past 20 years I have learnt a lot about man and his ways and God's relationship with him. I have learnt a lot about myself too, and the kind of relationship God wants with me. One of the things that really surprised me was just how much good God could bring out of a seemingly hopeless situation. Here in the midst of the worst nightmare I had ever experienced, and at one of my lowest points, God grants me the desire I had held in my heart since the age of 12 or 13 years, the desire to write. So here I am writing my testimony as He commanded. It is fitting that He gets the glory.

Pride and Humility

···•●•···

Though I met and married my husband here in England, his home was the islands of Trinidad and Tobago. This is where we headed for our honeymoon and it was my first experience of island living as an adult. England had been my home since I was 5 years old. I had only snapshot images of life in Jamaica and had not been back since.

I loved my time in Trinidad. The sun, sand, people and the food were all great. However, there were a few occasions when certain foods and drinks held little appeal. One occasion that I remember clearly was when I was presented with a bowl of porridge called 'flour pap' for breakfast; his grandmother prepared it. I ate it and made polite enquiry into its ingredients and method of preparation but in my heart I thought badly of it and wondered how anyone could eat such poor fare. I ate with apparent satisfaction and said all that was proper, while looking down my nose at the meal, which was indeed below my own standards, and not at all what I was used to.

We often forget that God is omniscient that He knows our thoughts. He certainly knew mine. Later that year we returned to Trinidad to lead a small church. My husband's salary was adequate and met our needs with a bit of economy. However, being a small church with only a small number of people in full-time employment, tithes and offerings were not always sufficient to meet the church bills and pay his salary. On these occasions the bills were paid first so that we did not receive a full wage. The congregation however were very generous and we frequently received gift parcels of food that supplemented the low wage. They wanted to bless us, and they truly did. Their gifts did not supply us with luxuries, but were enough for our needs.

As I remember, one particular month was more difficult than usual. We had received a little over half our salary and there was about another 10 days before the next wage. Our food supply was low. We had no money and I struggled to produce meals, until finally, a new day dawned. I opened the cupboards to see what was available to prepare breakfast. My husband already knew food was low, and we had prayed about it. I found a little flour, a little powdered milk, and a sprinkling of sugar, absolutely nothing else anywhere. What could I do with this? I looked at them for a long while knowing my husband would be leaving for work soon, and as I looked, I remembered our honeymoon and the porridge we'd had one morning. I was thankful I'd taken instructions on the making of it, and although I did not have any of the spices to make it more palatable, the basic ingredients were there. I cooked the porridge, laid the table and served it. It was just enough for two. As we gave thanks for the meal, I told my husband it was the last of our supplies. He seemed worried, but strangely, I was not. This was due partly to the memory of God's promise to me that I'd be safe with Him, and partly because I always trusted Him to know His own business. I knew that He was aware of our need and felt that this might be a test of my faith and dependence on Him. Either way I knew God would make a way. I began to eat and as I raised the first spoonful to my mouth, God took me on a journey backward in time to the morning 16-18 months previously when I had despised the porridge given to me. I saw myself in my pride and it was not a pretty sight.

God spoke to me then and told me that he had cut off all our supplies to bring me to that place where I would prepare and eat with thanksgiving that "poor" meal. I saw how greatly I had displeased Him to earn myself such a harsh lesson. I asked Him to forgive me and to help me never to be proud or think more highly of myself, or anything I owned, than I should. I ate my humble porridge and was satisfied. I cleared the table and washed up. As I waved my husband goodbye and he walked off toward the gate, a stranger carrying a box was walking toward our gate and called out to us. He came into the yard and up the shallow step onto the veranda (patio) and followed my husband into the living room where he placed the box on the floor. We then exchanged greetings and he introduced himself as the Pastor from the neighbouring village. He apologised that he had not had time to visit us before to welcome us to the area, and proceeded to tell us that during his devotion hour (prayer time) the previous evening, God directed him to prepare a box of groceries for us. He did this with his wife's help. He took an envelope containing $45 from his breast pocket and gave it to us. I did not feel relief that God had provided because I knew He would. What I did feel, however, was that I had been severely disciplined by a Just God. I remembered His words that He had "cut off" our supplies to teach me a lesson. Having done so and accepted my remorse and forgiven me, He had opened the doors for our supplies again. As though to prove the point, not that God needs to prove anything, three times during that same day, various members popped in for a chat, as was their custom, bringing some groceries, none a duplicate of what I had already received. That lesson was burnt on my heart. God chastises those He loves. I know beyond a shadow of doubt that He loves me. God cannot lie. Pride really does come before a fall, but humility and repentance bring forgiveness and restoration.

Pregnancy and how I coped

···●●···

We had decided on the number of children we wanted before we married...well, sort of. I think I'd wanted five and my husband, four. I was from a family of eight children and we had been very happy and had had hilarious times, so I wanted to offer our children the same on a smaller scale. In any case, we both agreed at the time that whatever number of children we had, one should be adopted. My body clock brought our plans forward by about one year and we tried to start a family. We prayed and still nothing happened. I was more anxious about it than he was. In fact, he wasn't anxious at all and took everything in his stride, so to speak.

So then, there we were, over two years married, trying for a child for little over a year without success. I began to wonder if one of us had a problem, or if I really was just too anxious about it and needed to relax and let nature take its course. By this time my body clock was going crazy, that strong desire for fulfilment in motherhood became more overwhelming with each passing month. I became upset and tearful but hid these facts from my husband. I had also begun to talk myself round to the idea that we might have to adopt all our children (yes, I was a drama queen). I knew children were a gift from God. It could be that He was withholding this particular gift so that we could give a home to other children. If that was the case, I was willing, but I would so love to have a child of my own. I felt as if my soul cried for it also. I had arranged to see my GP to discuss our difficulties and see what he advised. My husband was aware of my intention, we had talked about it and I suppose he knew I needed to feel that I was doing something positive about it. This visit to the doctor was that first step in actively doing.

I had been blessed with regular monthly cycles (like clockwork) so on the morning of my appointment, even with allowances for a late appearance, I knew it was no longer necessary as I was pregnant. You women will understand what I mean. I kept my appointment anyway and walked into the doctor's office with a smile on my face and told him I was pregnant. He was the first to know. When in response to his enquiry, I informed him of the date of my last cycle, he told me that it was too soon to know if I was pregnant and booked another appointment for a month's time. I was annoyed and ignored his comment. What did he know? I went back anyway and he confirmed my condition, not that I needed it by that time.

It wasn't long before morning sickness (24hr morning sickness) took over and I was wishing the pregnancy elsewhere. None of the books and baby magazines had prepared me for this and I felt that someone ought to be sued for withholding the truth. I'd expected 'morning' sickness and some minor discomforts, but nothing like this. I was miserable, and was transformed from a meek lamb into a dragon. My poor husband was, metaphorically, eaten alive, chewed over and spat out more times than I care to remember by my suddenly very sharp tongue. Poor man. It's no surprise that when I suggested we tried for a second child a few years later that he refused point blank. Self-preservation must have been uppermost in his mind. It took me a while to realise this and I was beginning to despair of his ever changing his mind, however, that's another story.

My days and nights were an equal mix of nausea, insomnia, hunger, sickness and retching.

Added to this was an aversion to food and drink; its appearance, smell, touch/feel, taste, texture, etc. I had to empty the cupboards and throw it all out. There was nothing in the house but a bottle of milk, a box of cornflakes and water, which I could tolerate in extremely small amounts, and separately. Little sips of ice-cold milk or water and a spoon full of dry cornflakes. I could keep those offerings down provided I did not smell my neighbours' food on the boil, or come into contact with food of any kind when I ventured out. I walked with my eyes on the ground and would quickly look away if I caught sight of a scrap of food, even a wrapper. Of course, once out in the community, my nostrils were constantly assaulted by the rich scents of the Caribbean mingled with over-ripe fruit, car fumes and the spicy aroma of a cooking pot. I was very, very, miserable. During this period my husband had most of his meals out to spare me the discomforts of trying to prepare one. He could not approach me if he had recently eaten, as the smell of food on his breath would cause me to heave – that's how bad it was.

At about the same time, my salivary glands went into mass production and getting rid of the stuff was not as easy as you may think. It was a nightmare, a logistic minefield of planning, and a conversation stopper. I must admit that during this period, I doubt very much that I was a good wife, good Christian, good anything. I was brimful with self-pity. Each 24hr was a challenge that I would pass on if I could and this went on for the first five months of pregnancy. Even before the pregnancy was confirmed, if I wore a skirt or anything that was fitted around the waist I would feel as though hands were around my throat. So I was in maternity wear even without a bump to show to save me from losing my mind. And all this time I'm thinking, "serves me right for wanting a baby". I also thought that if when this baby made their way into the world they gave me any cheek, boy, would they be sorry, after what I was going through.

Then one day a wonderful change took place, I had a craving for mangoes and they were in plentiful supply. I was also able to eat small amounts of food if it was not too spicy, dry foods were preferable. Unfortunately another unwelcomed change, which had been growing gradually over the weeks, had fully materialised and had to be acknowledged. I looked at my husband one day and wondered how on earth I had ever come to marry him. I thought surely my mum or brothers, or someone should have stopped me, what had been the attraction? This was very upsetting for both of us as he had realised that I was avoiding him and was very hurt (any wonder!). I didn't know where to turn for help except to my Doctor. Not a very good decision I thought initially because, having explained this terrible position I found myself in and bursting into tears in his presence, in his practice (very humiliating), he leant back in his chair and chuckled ever so softly, but chuckle he did, and me, the supersensitive being I had become, could tell that he wanted to laugh out loud! I thought, "Why did I ever bother to tell you anything? You're a man just like my husband, and I don't like you either!" Offended, I glared at him and he apologised and went on to explain that it was all due to my hormones being "up the creek". He had never heard of such strong aversions as I was experiencing, but assured me I should not worry too much as things would settle back to normal in no time. He said I should return with my husband so he could explain it to us both. We didn't return, but we were both *so* relieved to know we had not made a dreadful mistake. My family was exonerated.

We waited anxiously for the hormones to 'settle' and until they did, avoided each other. You can see why he refused to even contemplate a second pregnancy, but as I said, that's another story. The doctor had not lied, and one day, I looked and saw all the reasons I'd married my husband apart from his being tall, dark and...I was even able to cook meals and eat them – things were on the up. The wife he'd married was back. The only times I slid into the old ways was when he came home without a bag of mangoes. This was totally unacceptable, and he would have to go out again or face the music. At times, I had a little insight into my behaviour, but I could not help myself. I didn't just *want* mangoes, I *needed* them, and I don't care what anyone says about eating for one. It's not true, not where mangoes or any other craving is concerned. I could not think straight or sleep if, when I wanted a mango, I could not have one, and I generally wanted at least 2 on the hour, almost every hour day and night. It was the strangest thing and it made me a stranger to myself. I sort of looked on and wondered who that woman was that was behaving so terribly.

The joy of pregnancy was a stranger to me until the last two and a half to three months.

Prior to this, I think I'd even forgotten to give thanks for answered prayers, because almost from day one I was struggling with the side effects.

Living in Trinidad as we did, I had none of my family near. At a time like that, a girl wants her mother close by. I felt the distance then. All my family were in the UK. I'd written to tell my mum the good news and got lots of congrats from everyone. My sister who was a midwife sent me lots of information and tips. But the one thing I wanted and did not think I would get was to have my mum with me for the birth, and for practical advice. What did I know about being a mother? I thought of my older sister and my sisters'-in-law (all three of them), and the fact that my mum had been there for them, one way or another, but I would be on my own. I felt sad about it. Mum did not like travelling by air so I resisted the urge to ask her to come to me. I did not even hope she would come either. I just hoped God would help me to do the right thing and re-mind me of those things I had learnt and ob-served my mother doing for my younger brother and sisters. I was not overly con-cerned, motherhood was supposed to be a nat-ural, instinctive process after all but her support would have been welcomed and an added security.

I always looked forward to mail that had an air letter amongst them. I would work my way through the other stuff and leave the air letter last, so I could savour the anticipation of its content and news of home. One day, the letter was from my mum and she was coming to Trinidad. My mum who really and truly did not like travelling by air, was coming to Trinidad to be with me. And, she was coming for *six weeks*. I read it over and over again for days, weeks, and even as I write, I can still feel the thrill, the joy, and emotion of knowing how much she had demonstrated her love for me by that one act. Hard on the heels of those thoughts was the knowledge that God loved me so much. He was sending my mother to me and I would not be alone, because that is how I'd felt despite being surrounded by people who loved me. I suppose when you want your mum; no one else will do in quite the same way.

Her timing was great. She arrived four days before her granddaughter was born, was present for her blessing, gave me all the advice and practical help I needed, and by the time she left to return home, I felt I was a veteran, an old hand at motherhood. Thanks mum.

Motherhood

···•●•···

If you are a mother, you know how fascinated you can become with your growing, moving and sometimes sticking-out bump. I loved grasping the protruding arm or leg and feeling it shy away only to appear somewhere else. I remember thinking, "this child is her father's daughter", never still for a moment. She was particularly active after a session of jazz or gospel music. Her dad regularly stopped me from continuing what I was doing because he felt the need to share his music with his daughter. Forget all the housework waiting to be done; he would place headphones on my bump so she could listen. It felt like she was turning cartwheels or performing flips, and while I rejoiced in these signs of a healthy baby, I was frequently just gasping for breath as a limb was thrust upwards into my diaphragm.

I couldn't wait for her to make her big entry (of course, I didn't know I was having a girl and secretly hoped for a boy, though her father insisted he was having a daughter). I was slowly accumulating an assortment of baby products and clothes, all in neutral colours, and had also bought two-dozen terry towels and one dozen muslin nappies (disposables were restricted to special occasions, days out or long periods away from home). I took great delight in washing those nappies, hanging them out on the clothesline, and watching them glisten in the sunlight as they wafted to and fro in the gentle Caribbean breeze. When they were joined by an assortment of doll-sized baby wear, I felt I had fulfilled my purpose for being. I was a child of God, a daughter, a wife and now mother. My joy knew no end.

I went into labour at 5.30am and arrived at the hospital at 7am on a Wednesday morning, and she made her arrival at 5.45p.m. that day. I must admit, there was a time when I thought I would not make it. Eve has *a lot* to answer for. When the midwife informed me I had a little girl, I felt disappointment rising but it quickly evaporated into nothingness when, a split second later, I saw her beautiful face and felt an emotion beyond description, that defies words, rise from some place I had no knowledge of and take possession of my soul. Hard on the heels of this emotion was the knowledge that she was mine. At no time were the role of God the giver, or my husband and equal player, granted credence. She was gorgeous, she was beautiful, I had brought her into this world and she was mine. I had done this. I was besotted.

This state of affairs could not be allowed to continue, so my baby was whisked away to the nursery and I was informed that the doctor would be in shortly as I required stitches. Shortly turned out to be nearly 3hrs later during which time I received little or no attention, did not see my baby or her father who had been sent away and told to return in the morning, as he informed me when he came. All this took place in the new, state of the art maternity hospital. Unfortunately for me and several other expectant mothers, we had chosen to give birth when cricket, a national passion, was being played on the islands (England v West Indies) and a good proportion of the staff including midwives and paediatricians had 'followed' the game (at short/no notice) to another island. I clearly remember the midwife examining me and saying "if you feel like pushing, don't, it's not time yet" and leaving me to attend another mother-to-be. So, I panted and carried out the breathing exercises I could remember, and wondered what was going on. This was not what I had been told would happen; my husband and mother were not permitted to be with me. They were waiting outside, and I was anxious on my own.

After several hours with an occasional head round the door, the midwife again carried out an examination and this time said, "When you feel like you want to go to the toilet, push". She said it with emphasis and promptly left the room as before. It wasn't long before I wanted to push, but I wasn't going to without the midwife present, so I rang for her and panted instead. Several contractions and pants later she came, checked me and told me to push, but still she left me and I was too scared to obey, not knowing what might happen with no-one to help. Whether because I did not push or some other problem, there were complications and I wound up with the full compliment of maternity staff assisting me to give birth (paediatrician and 2 midwives). God alone knows what happened to the other women deprived of support while I was attended to. I couldn't spare them a thought. I was in a world of unspeakable torture from which there was no relief. I thought I would surely die from the pain despite the assurance given in the Word (woman being spared in childbirth and all that jazz – some sparing I thought!). I concluded that childbirth, for me, was a trip to hell and back, and took time out to make my peace with God, and ask him to spare the baby and look after my husband. Who'd have thought I'd live to tell the tale.

Eventually I was, with others, escorted to the ward and placed on a unit for mothers who'd had caesarean deliveries, as there was no 'room at the inn'. By now it was gone ten o'clock and I had not seen my baby. Each time I asked I was told she was ok and in the nursery. As I was in the Caribbean and not the UK, I was not sure what to expect but did not think this separation could be right and waited helplessly for someone to bring her to me. Having been admitted to the ward and seeing the other mothers with their babies, I began to suspect that something was very wrong and tried desperately not to worry. Each time I'd asked for her to be brought, giving my details, the nurses would express surprise that I had not seen her all those hours and went off, I thought to get her, but did not return. I was numb, prepared myself for the worst and had decided that she had died and they were waiting for my husband to return to inform me of it. You can imagine my scepticism and relief when finally at about

11.15p.m. the night nurse who was new on duty listened to my problem and returned placing a bundle in my arms. I looked at the baby not expecting to see my baby and wondering which mother they had pleaded with to borrow their baby to appease me (I had great imagination). I recognised her instantly but it took a moment for me to acknowledge that this was indeed my own daughter and when I finally allowed my heart to accept that truth, all the pent-up emotions were released and tears flooded my eyes and ran like a waterfall down my face. I could not stem the flow or blink them away, afraid to take my eyes off her for even a moment. The midwife sat next to me and hugged and rocked me as I cried. She later brought me a mug of tea, which was only the second time sustenance had passed my lips since my mum had made me a cup of tea that morning before leaving for the hospital. Only then did I realise how hungry I was. I slept fitfully that night, overcome with fascination and relief.

In the morning mother and baby were declared fit, I packed my bag and waited for my husband; I could not wait to get away and was home by 10am. When I got home, mum prepared a full English breakfast at my request and I polished it off, not a trace of it was left on the plate. But before I left the hospital, the most amazing thing happened that I still remember as though it were yesterday. I recall that throughout my pregnancy, my husband gave our daughter a running commentary of his days and shared his music with her (all via my belly button) and he always addressed her by name. I used to worry that if it were a boy he might be confused by it all. Well, on this day, and less than 1 day old, I got her washed, dressed and wrapped in a blanket, 'swaddling' style, arms securely tucked in as you do, or did in those days. When I was informed that my husband had arrived and was waiting in the lounge area, I picked her up and held her to me and walked out to meet him. Still several paces away he smiled at me and said "Good morning Nadya". Holding her as I did, her back toward him, at the sound of his voice she began to wriggle and grunt and push with her arms and legs while straining her head back and around toward him. With one last grunt and thrust she got her arms free and turning to him she opened them wide, looked up at him as he stooped forward and said "eh". She held on to his finger as babies do but conversed as no 14hr 50min baby should, and that was it! I was out of the picture and just watched in amazement as her "eh eh" echoed to his enquiries on her health and thoughts on what it was like to finally be here. They remained inseparable for years and I did not get a look-in until her mid to late teens.

Did I tell you I informed my husband that our family was now complete, and I would not go through the trauma of labour again? I did not believe God intended me to suffer so, and that if I truly loved myself, which is important if I am to love others, then I could not subject myself to such pain ever again. He took it on the chin like a man (where else?) and calmly informed me that his daughter was enough for him.

You know, I am not a reader of magazines and their problem pages but after the birth of our daughter I would buy and read magazines on mother and baby, parenting, etc. mostly to see what they said. I felt and still believe that parenting is generally instinctive and that we learn from our parents and those who have gone before and add their knowledge to what appears to come naturally. I went through a phase where these magazines seemed to be full of articles about parents who regretted having only one child and children who regretted not having siblings to play with. Their stories were so sad and there seemed to be a lot of pain expressed, especially amongst those where it was choice and not medical complications that had guided their decisions. I looked at my daughter and thought, "how can I put her through that?". Even though my decision to have more children was not based on that, it got me thinking about the big family we had talked about; and as my mother said when I asked how she'd managed to have eight children (4boys, 4girls), "Its' a forgetful pain", and she's right, I forgot.

Did I tell you that at less than two days old our daughter was hung-over? And if you're wondering who the culprit was, yes, it was me. I had a mug of warm milk, a spoonful of honey, and a teaspoonful of brandy (my night cap). I had been prescribed warm milk and honey to treat insomnia during the pregnancy. It worked a treat. I had also had a craving for this drink with a drop of brandy for some weeks and had naturally resisted. So, when I felt the craving again I only remember thinking, "Thank goodness I'm not pregnant anymore". I'd had this drink on my first and second night home from the hospital. I was breast-feeding and it hadn't occurred to me that it might affect my milk – I just did not think about it. The poor child lived in a drunken haze for 3-4 days barely able to stay awake long enough for a feed, and then what a feed! It was on the third evening when my mother saw me reach for the brandy that she realised why our daughter was sleeping so much. I was mortified and felt *so* guilty and worried that I may have harmed her. Whenever I thought of it, I could not help laughing inwardly. Not very proper I know, but no harm done, thank God.

I quickly fell into a routine and I think surprised mum with how well I'd adjusted to motherhood (except for the brandy affair). Before she left Trinidad she warmly professed her love for me, and with the same warmth, informed me that, "if yuh children nuh have nuh manners, yuh cyan come inna me house", to translate, "If your children are not well behaved, you're not welcome in my house". Mum always slipped into the vernacular when she felt something keenly or wanted to make a point. POINT TAKEN. Discipline would not be, and was not withheld, for while a return to England seemed like a distant dream, what were dreams for if not to have them and hope? My husband often thought I was too unyielding but I don't think he quite understood the gravity of mum's words, and she is a woman of her word. No-one, and nothing, was going to keep me out of mum's house. Both grandchildren are a credit to her today.

I missed her once she'd gone, but occupied my time well, or so I thought, treating Nadya like a living doll. I went from a round of dressing her up and combing little ringlets in her hair, to simply holding, feeding and marvelling at her perfection. Each day seemed to vanish as in a puff of smoke and a new one began. Now on a few occasions on his return from work, my husband would go into the kitchen, open empty pots and rummage through the fridge and appear with a sandwich and drink or snack of some kind. I thought nothing of it, until one particular evening when having gone through the same routine and come out empty handed, he approached me with an edge to his voice and asked if there was to be any dinner?

"Dinner?" I thought aloud, and looked at him in innocent amazement wondering why he would want to eat. With a hint of annoyance or irritation he gave me a crooked smile and said "life goes on you know".

"I know that", I said wondering what he was talking about. Enlightenment was around the corner. He informed me, by now very kindly and gently, that he understood fully why I was so wrapped up in Nadya because she was a beautiful baby, but "we must eat". He had my attention now and when he confessed that after a long day at work he was hungry. I felt terrible for I looked at him and saw it was the truth. I smile at the memory now, but was quite shocked to realise that for 2-3 days I had not cooked. I am not sure that I had eaten anything and had not felt the need for food. Motherhood filled me. At the time it was my food. I felt I needed nothing else. He saw my plight and sat me down to give me a mini sermon on appreciating the gift more than the giver and warned me of the sin of idolatry, our precious baby being my idol. He was right, I saw it all and was shocked at myself and ashamed that having prayed for and been blessed with a child, I had made the mistake of putting her before my relationship with God and my husband. I begged both their pardon and got up to prepare a meal.

I made sure dinner was ready when he arrived home each day, and I asked God to guard me against ever placing anyone or anything before him in my estimation. Thank God for the gentle correction of my husband. I learned a valuable lesson that day and it has remained in the forefront of my thinking in every situation and new relationships I have forged. All that I am and all that I have, is from God and is an expression of His love for me. How could I value the expression of love more than the one whose expression it is? God has been extravagant in expressing His love for me over the years. He leaves no room for doubt. What can separate me from the love of God?

Did I meet an Angel?

··•●•··

Our daughter was about six months old when I had an experience that I doubt I will ever forget. It was mid-morning and I had not long put her to bed for a rest. I did not expect her to sleep, she never did even at that young age, but it was a routine I had put in place whether she liked it or not. I was wearing a cotton lounger (a loose fitting button-through robe, sort of like a glorified dressing gown), a common daytime attire for the warm climes of the Caribbean, suitable for wearing within the boundaries of the home only, and was busy with the housework when I heard the local call of greeting, "Ohh dee". (I've no idea if it's a proper word; a derivative of another, how it's spelt or anything, this is my own personal, phonetic, attempt). I was in the open plan living area with the sliding glass doors leading to the veranda. I paused and waited, not sure if the call was for me, or my neighbour. It came again, "Ohh dee", and I went out to the veranda to see who it was.

Looking down (our home was built on pillars with external steps) I saw an Indian man

(60+) with low cut greying and thinning hair, and a cheerful but weary smile looking up at me. He was short in stature and standing just within the boundary of the property on the overgrown drive. His overall appearance was pleasant. I did not recognise him and thought he might want direction. He looked hot and tired, his feet, brown leather sandals and the hem of his black trousers were dusty, as though he had been on a long journey, and he wore a beige shirt-jack (a cross between a shirt and jacket as its name implies, but made of lightweight poly-cotton material, short-sleeved, embroidered, loose fitting and very typical casual dress for Trinidad). I responded, "Good morning, can I help you?" He asked if I could bring him a glass of water and I invited him to come up and take a seat on the veranda out of the sun. I watched as he slowly made his way along the drive, disappear under the house and emerged at the bottom step to make his way up. Even as I heard the invitation leave my mouth I was wondering what I was doing inviting a stranger into my home with-out my husband present to protect us. I watched him closely as he made his way, try-ing to gauge whether or not he was likely to pose a risk in which case I would lock myself and our daughter in the house before he got to the top of the steps, and call for help. I did not sense any danger in this tired old man and invited him to take a seat. I enquired if he would prefer a glass of cool aid (juice), but he chose water with ice and I had a glass of juice to join my guest.

We sat on the veranda with the door only partially closed so I could hear the baby, and had a drink. He drank thirstily and I poured him another glass of water. He leant back in the chair and sighed and just looked about for a while. I had lots of questions but being shy, felt tongue-tied and wondered what to say. He seemed comfortable in the silence so I said nothing and waited. It was strange but I felt comfortable and I wondered at this. He asked for my name, wanted to know where I was from and how I came to be living there. I found myself answering without any reservations and all the while wondering why I was doing this and who this man was. When my mind tried to enforce caution (and I am generally a cautious person) my heart responded and my mouth spoke. He asked about my husband and the work he did, and I explained that he was a local pastor. He seemed very interested in us, what we did and why, where we came from etc. and there I was volunteering information as though I had known this man all my life. I was at ease with him. One thing that I have never forgotten is that his keen bright eyes were at variance to his whole tired, almost drooping persona, and that again and again I was drawn to those eyes. I would first study those eyes, which were at once open, yet gave nothing away, and then take in the rest of him and think, this does not fit. Yet I was not sure what it was that was odd, strange but not threatening. I don't know if he realised that I was scrutinising him. He was totally at ease.

When he had finished his drink, I fully ex-pected him to leave but instead he took up a position of complete relaxation and looked about him at the scenery. I was surprised and a bit taken aback, this was going beyond what I thought was socially acceptable behaviour. I took the tray away and returned and sat with him. He wanted to know about the community and all sorts. I don't know what else we talked about but we did for hours, literally, like we were old friends. I even offered him lunch, which he refused but invited me to have mine, while he accepted a glass of juice and we ate/drank and chatted away. He even met our daughter who'd had enough quiet time and let me know it. All the while I kept thinking what a strange happening this was, and hoped my husband would come home, which he sometimes did in the middle of the day, to meet this nice but strange old man. The only thing I found out about him was that he was not from Kelly Village; he was passing through on his way from...? To...? Which isn't a great deal you must admit in over two hours of conversation. I felt he knew everything that was worth knowing about me, and my life in Trinidad.

I felt regret when he eventually rose to leave. I had enjoyed my time with him, but could not explain the sense of loss I felt. It was totally unreasonable and irrational for someone I had just met. I'd had this feeling that he knew me and knew of me all the while we'd spoken, and I'd tried to place his face. Had I met him before somewhere? Is that how he knew me? But I had not; his was not the kind of face (eyes, persona) you forgot. I mumbled that I would get my slippers and show him out but he waved this idea away and said that if he could find his way up, then he could as easily make his way out. In other words, "don't trouble yourself". I accepted this and just stood and watched him begin to make his way down the steps. Before he was half way down I picked up the tray, rushed through to the kitchen and placed it by the sink and went out again to wave him off. Looking over the balcony and just under the house where I expected him to emerge, I waited more than the few seconds it should have taken him with his slow, slightly slouching gait. When he didn't show, I looked to the road only briefly because there is no way he could have gone that far and then looked down again. Maybe he had stopped under the house to catch his breath or do up his sandals. When still he did not emerge, I became just a little anxious and wondered if he was as harmless as I had thought, or was he hiding and waiting to come up again to steal? Or...Who knows? I looked long and hard up and down the road including the side street; from the veranda I had a clear view for some distance. If he were on the road, I would see him but how he could have got there so quickly, only God knew.

Not seeing him, I prayed, asked God to protect the baby and me and quickly went downstairs, fully expecting to see him leaning against one of the pillars that supported the house. He was nowhere in sight and I could not understand where he could have got to. I walked around foolishly checking each pillar, walked up the drive to the road looking in both directions,

around the corner and looking down the
"trace" (street), no sign of him and there were
very few people about to obscure my view. My
heart was pounding by this time and I ran
back under the house and up the steps to the
veranda and looked again; maybe, somehow I
had missed him, but he wasn't there. I re-
traced my actions, timing, how long it may
have taken for me to take the tray to the
kitchen and back; long enough for him to get
to the bottom of the steps, just, but not out
from under the building, and certainly not off
the property, let alone out of sight! My heart
began to beat faster as I picked up my daughter and walked about the living room and then
onto the veranda looking at the chair where
he'd sat looking at the ring of water on the
patio table left by the glass he drank from,
wondering, searching for a reasonable explanation.

The passage about entertaining angels una-
ware in the bible popped into my mind, and
just as quickly, I tried to throw it out, but it
would not go. Like rewinding a film, I went
through the greeting, meeting, conversation,
and my uncharacteristic behaviour; the sense
of knowing, of his knowing, of being safe. I'd
had the sense that the alertness, keenness,

youthful but agelessness of his eyes, belied his mature stature, his age. All these thoughts and more had assaulted my mind the whole time we had talked. I had found it puzzling and disconcerting, and now this, he had vanished. Now I know I have a vivid imagination, but I did not accept this. There had to be a reasonable explanation, I just could not find it!

I began to wonder if I'd had a special visitor and decided that if I had, thank God I had not refused to give him water, and thank goodness I had offered him lunch out of the little I had and rest and shelter from the sun. Even while I thought along this vein, a part of me was also thinking that I must be crazy for thinking like that, but the thoughts did not leave me and his disappearance only reinforced them. I thought when I told my husband about this incident that his basic good sense would clear the whole thing up for me but it didn't. To say, "He must have gone somewhere?" did not help because I knew he did not have the time to go anywhere, at least, not as we measure time. My husband advised me to be more careful whom I invited in when he was not around. I agreed wholeheartedly.

The situation has never risen again. I have never seen that man again, though I've looked for him. I have never felt that way about anyone again. So the question is...was he man or angel? Maybe one day I'll have my answer, but whatever it is, that day is recorded as one of the most memorable experience of my life.

Back to work

·· • ● • ··

Although I trained as a Dental Technician here in the UK between 1976 and 1979, I did not complete my qualification until 1985, having failed one of four components of the City & Guilds award. The death of my father, shortly after my 21st birthday, as I prepared for my final examinations massively discouraged me, and I suddenly lacked all motivation to achieve academically. I was striving for him, so I could hear him say well done. Art was my first love, but he had put an end to that dream, as he could not see a useful/profitable career coming out of the study of it. He was a practical man and I was a dreamer who wanted to study art for the joy of it, with no thought of how it could be used to finance my life. "Ambition" was an important word in his vocabulary, and we were encouraged to have and achieve our own (if it were practical or sensible). As much as I enjoyed the work of a dental technician, I chose this career because it allowed some room for my artistic traits and I loved to use my hands. My "ambition", if you can call it that, was to get married, have children and care for family and home. To me, everything else was secondary. I would have worked at any unskilled job to meet the needs of my family if need be. Of course, I could not tell my parents this, so I dutifully chose and worked at carving out a career for myself, but my heart was not in it. It was just something one did, and I saw that it was a useful thing to have a career.

Within a year of our marriage we moved lock, stock and barrel to Trinidad and I set about finding a job as a dental technician. I went to several interviews and the fact that I had not completed my studies did not seem to be an issue. I was offered two or three jobs, but could not accept them because I found the working arrangements in those laboratories very different from those practiced in the UK. I would be exposing myself, and patients to risks that were unacceptable. I was expected to have direct contact with patients and build up my own clientele, a thing not done in the UK.

Discouraged, I worked as a receptionist for an optometrist, and later as an Optical Technician. I had given up work a month before our daughter was due (no maternity leave) and was in no hurry to return. I loved being a mother. With her birth, I had realised my ambition completely.

Finances were usually tight, but now with an 8-month old baby in the picture, I could not afford the luxury of being a housewife any longer. It was time to return to work.

From about the age of 14 years I had always enjoyed looking through the job columns of the newspapers. Even when happily employed I continued the habit; the birth of our daughter had not changed anything. Jobs for Dental Technicians were rarely advertised in Trinidad, even those I had applied for had been by scouring the equivalent of our yellow pages, and contacting the laboratories listed. In the 3 years since moving to Trinidad and going through the job section of the papers, jobs fitting the description I sought were few and far between, and none suitable for my training had ever been advertised to my knowledge.

We had agreed that I would return to work and so I had already arranged childcare. All I needed was the job. As stated above, I had worked as a receptionist and an optical technician but never as a dental technician. I was determined that my years of training should not be wasted any longer, but where would I find suitable employment? On this particular Thursday morning I woke up and prayed. I told God of our need for me to work. I told Him of my desire to use my training and of the dearth of jobs to allow this. I asked Him to provide me with such a job. I thanked Him, fully confident that He'd heard and would answer my prayer. I began my day; breakfast, see my husband off to work, housework, care for our daughter. I was now free to look at the job section of the paper. I went directly to column 'D' and scrolled down looking for 'Dental' then past 'R' for Receptionist, past 'S' for Surgeon and there it was 'T' for Technician, the only one, the right one – I was stunned! I always expect God to hear and answer, but often the speed at which He does so amazes me. I stared at it, that job was mine and no one else could have it. It was placed there for me. I was so excited, I responded to the advert immediately and was asked to attend an interview that very afternoon. I then rang the office to share the news with my husband and asked him to escort me to the interview arranged for 4pm. I got the job even though I had no experience of working with crowns and bridges except in training (I had worked exclusively with dentures and in the last year before moving to Trinidad, with artificial prostheses – eyes, orbits and ears, which brought out the artist in me). He was willing to train me on the job so I was asked to start the following Monday. I agreed to this as childcare had already been arranged.

Arriving home, I enquired into our finances because I had already calculated that I would need $60 (T&T dollars) a week for transport. We had none. We had food in the cupboards; petrol in the car and it would be another week before my husband would receive his salary. Our most immediate need was for milk and a few necessities for our daughter and of course transport for me to get to work. I had a word with God about this but was not unduly concerned because He knew all these things, had provided the job and would provide all I needed to do it. So, whenever I thought about our needs, I just thanked God and went about my daily routines.

Friday came and went with no change in our finances. On Saturday I completed my usual routine and with the baby in tow, went for a walk through the village to pass the time with whomever I met on the way. This is called "lyming", and is a common social practice that I had finally come to grips with and enjoyed. I chatted to several people on the way and eventually ended with our daughter's godmother and her family. She was pleased to see us because I had saved her a journey. She had a gift for her goddaughter, a dress, and one for me, an envelope containing $45. When asked about the money, if it was for her goddaughter, she responded that she had felt led to give me a gift of money after a time of prayer on the previous evening. I thanked her and God and on the journey home bought the things our daughter needed, leaving $30 towards my transport costs. I asked God to continue to provide my needs and He did, though not in the way I had imagined he would.

Several amazing things happened during that first week of work and all but one, were never repeated again. One morning, as I stood waiting for the taxi by the gate, I saw a car coming and stuck my hand out as you would for a bus here in England. It stopped and the driver asked where I was headed for – standard procedure – and I replied that I was going to the capital Port of Spain. He leant across the seat to open the door and I got in. We chatted all the way but I thought it strange that he did not stop at the taxi rank to take on passengers. I asked if he "was a taxi" – a local expression, regular cars are registered for use as taxi's, like our mini cab service. He replied that he was, but was not working in that capacity that morning because he had business to conduct in town (Port of Spain). I watched the route closely however for any diversion that might indicate possible danger. When we arrived and I proffered the $6 fare for the two stages of my journey that he had completed, he refused payment, as he was not "on duty". On another occasion, the taxi that I took to town for the second stage of my journey also completed the third stage and took me to work. But the driver, unknown to me, had actually ended his shift at the last stop in the town centre where he had collected fare from the alighting passengers. I thought I was his last passenger but he was in fact, on his way home so enquiring where I was heading and finding it to be on his way, he offered me a lift and would not accept payment for this leg of the journey ($2). On two occasions the taxi was driven by the father of one of our church members, so he refused to accept the fare. One morning, the bus arrived just as I got to the main road in front of our home. The bus service was notorious for its' lack of timekeeping, which was why it was included in my return journey plan, but had not been included in my morning transportation plans. This was my third morning on the job and the first and only time I'd been fortunate enough to get the bus that week. The fare for the first part of my journey was only 50 cents; I was able to connect with another bus for the second part of my journey – also 50cents –and the third part was completed by taxi as usual. Catching the bus that morning meant a saving of $5. I can't remember all the instances when I saved money, but these examples stood out in my mind and by the end of my first week of work, I had $6 in my purse even though I'd started out with only $30 where $60 was required. I put what was left in the offering with thanksgiving and praise. I was paid weekly so now had the $60 I needed for transport and used it to the full. After that, I occasionally caught the bus and occasionally caught the taxi driven by our church member's father. The moral of this story is, like the miracle of the fish and the loaves, little can become much when you place it in Gods hand.

On Home Soil

··•●•··

The opportunity to return to England came in August 1984, and we took it. My husband was to teach at a Vocational Bible School in Birmingham and we were to be wardens of the student hostel, a beautiful manor house in Harbourne set in its' own grounds which had become the local recreation ground. We just had to step out of our back gate and we'd be in the park. It was a lovely setting for our daughter, who celebrated her second birthday there. She loved to go for walks and to the swings. Except for a six weeks Christmas job, I did not work for the year we spent there.

I was 26 years old, still shy, and a bit anxious about my position as the warden's wife. Surely wardens were older, even retired couples? At least that's the impression I'd had. I was a little older than some of the students, and possibly younger than a few. I stuck to what I knew best, which was to look after our home, a ground floor flat of palatial proportions, and left my husband to carry out the caretaking duties. In time, I got to know the students and we became a family of sorts. I loved to cook and made our own bread, cakes, biscuits, flapjacks and pizzas, especially pizzas weekly. I soon had regular visitors once the aroma wafted through the house, and I could not resist sharing it with them. It wasn't long before we came to an arrangement whereby, they would provide a bit of flour, or cheese, or eggs, or something from their meagre supplies, which I would add to our own and rustle up a tasty Friday or Saturday night meal for us all. Our daughter loved it when they came around as she was made a fuss of. It wasn't long before I had readymade childminders on tap; they'd just come and go off with her for hours on end. She loved it and she fascinated them because she was petite, doll sized, very clear at all times on what she wanted and inquisitive into the bargain, always questioning things...what is that? Why? Who made it? Who said? And every answer generated more questions.

During this period, I began to think about adding to our small family, but when I opened discussions with my husband, I was quite surprised that he showed no interest whatsoever and went so far as to inform me that he was very happy with his family as it was. I suggested that we might try for a son but he informed me that his daughter was all he wanted, "Thank you very much". To him, his family was complete – I was stunned. I know the day after her birth I had said something to that effect myself when I'd said I would not go through labour again, and I meant it at the time. It had been a shock to my system but I did not expect him to accept it so willingly. I spent months trying to persuade him to change his mind but he stood his ground firm-ly and I was quite distraught. No argument had any effect, he was adamant that his fami-ly was complete. One day, trying to hide my distress I stated clearly why I wanted to have another child and gave all the advantages and disadvantages, as I saw them, of not having an only child. He listened quietly, agreed with me, but looked worried as he gently informed me that he "could not go through another pregnancy". Puzzled, but relieved, I said, "Is that all? But it's not you that goes through the pregnancy, it's me". He'd looked at me, and then with a strange look in his eyes said, "I went through it too". My puzzlement grew and it was a moment or two before I realised what he meant. I understood then just how badly he had been affected by my hormonal changes and mood swings first time round. He'd rather have one child than run the risk of going through that again. He'd been hurt, and

I was so sorry. I did not speak of it again for some time and when I did, I tried to encourage him that all pregnancies were different, but he would not take the risk.

On a trip to London we stayed with my mum and I sought her advice and help. I spoke to my sister, the midwife, and I think they both encouraged him. Finally, he agreed and I became pregnant but miscarried at 10-12wks. We were advised to wait and allow my body to heal and strengthen itself before trying again so were surprised when in a matter of six weeks I was pregnant again. This time it was different; I was well throughout the entire pregnancy. I did not experience even a moment of morning sickness, thank God! The only undesirable change was that I found myself eating for England, Scotland and Wales. I was ravenously hungry 24hrs a day. I woke 2-3 times at night with hunger pangs. My bedside table resembled a snack bar. My handbag doubled in size and apart from my purse and a packet of tissues, it contained enough food and drink to keep me going when I had to go out. This was not a craving in the normal sense. I had experienced cravings with the first pregnancy and it hadn't been about hunger but about a strong, overwhelming desire for a particular food item. This was about very keen, overwhelming, hunger pangs, which left me feeling dizzy and weak-kneed, literally, when I attempted to resist eating and wait until the next meal. Needless to say, I gained an enormous amount of weight and was urged at the antenatal clinic to cut down. I'd prayed for a boy and thought, with an appetite like this, this baby must be a boy – very scientific.

It was during our year in Birmingham that my husband's dream of working in missions materialised with the founding of Mission Harambee, founded by him to fund our work in Kenya. I say our work, but mine revolved around the family and home while he was kept busy teaching, preaching, training local pastors, travelling within and outside the Kenyan borders spreading the gospel. We were its first and only missionaries. The headquarters of the organisation we worked with was based in Huruma on the edge of the largest slum in Nairobi. It was when we were courting that my husband had first shared his love for missions and made it clear that he would like to get involved in missions one day. I had promised God, when he'd first presented him to me, that I would not stand in the way of the work he called him to do. My supportive role as wife was very clear to me, and although I preferred to stay in England, wherever he was called, I would go happily.

By the time we were due to leave for Kenya I was four months pregnant and had no desire to have our baby abroad as my first experience of maternity services outside the UK had not inspired me with confidence. I wanted to be sure of what I could expect when I went into labour, and insisted that I remained here and joined him later. He agreed, and although he could not delay going to Kenya, our daughter and I stayed with my mother until I gave birth. I did ask him to stay, to put off our arrival in Kenya until the birth but he said it was not possible and had to go. I did think this odd considering the circumstances, but gave him the benefit of the doubt. Secretly, I thought he was anxious about my hormonal status and wanting a good reason to escape before I began to change and make his life a misery again.

With hindsight, staying to have our son in the UK was one of the best decisions I ever made. I had a very bad labour (I thought), it was touch and go for both of us in the end. Also, because I saw the labour ward where I might have given birth in Kenya when we visited a member of the fellowship. I concluded we would not have stood a chance, literally. I was horrified at what I found, and even more so when informed that it was commonplace.

Five minutes before we were due to watch Halley's Comet on TV (1986), and while playing a game of Black Jack with my brother to pass the time, I produced a mighty sneeze, one that I had been resisting for about 10 minutes, and my water broke, thrusting me into labour for a second time. All thought of the comet forgotten I dressed, grabbed my hospital bag and other paraphernalia and waited for the ambulance to arrive. On my way to the hospital, labour pains assaulted me and suddenly, all the horror of the process came flooding back; somehow... I had managed to forget it. "Oh no. What have I done?" were my secret thoughts, and this time round I was convinced I was several steps closer to my maker, and took time out to make my peace and entreat him on behalf of my husband, daughter and unborn child. This may all sound very melodramatic to you, but my mum can testify to God's grace that kept me here.

I eventually gave birth to a bouncing baby boy with cheeks like tennis balls and shoulders like an American footballer (padded). It was a little over a month before I recovered the full

use of my legs and could walk with a sem-
blance of normality. When he cried, someone
had to fetch him for me because by the time I
could get my feet to the floor he'd be in a tem-
per; and he was a mild tempered baby generally. My mum was a rock throughout; she stayed
with me through labour and was exhausted by
the end, but did not leave until she was sure
we were both OK.

I had taken his sister's 3-6 month old baby
grows to the hospital expecting them to be too
big (she had worn them at 8-9mths old) but
they did not fit him. The midwife tried everything I had and eventually gave up, put him in
a hospital nightdress and wrapped him in a
blanket. Mum rang my sister and she brought
her sons 6-9mth old clothing in; they just
about fitted.

In the end my husband had to return to England to escort us to Kenya as I could not make
the journey on my own with the children as
planned. Shortly after he arrived and we were
together with my mother, I suggested that
they should consider having me committed if I
were to ever mention wanting to have another
child, as it would be obvious that I had lost my
mind. There ended my dream, and his, of a
large(ish) family. This time we were both hap-

py with the decision. I thank God for our children; they are truly a blessing.

Languages

·· • ● • ··

1986 found us in Kenya with a new addition to our family, our son, only 2 months old and born at St Thomas' Hospital, London. Our daughter was 3½ yrs old but I don't think, apart from the early months of her life, that she ever really reflected her chronological age. This might be due to the exposure she received in the womb at the hands of her father, or maybe it was just that she had a more than usual enquiring mind. At first, she found life in Kenya puzzling and challenging, so her passion for questions knew no bounds. I sometimes felt my head would explode if she asked "why?" just one more time; I'll tell you of the master stroke of a plan I devised some years later to deal with the "why?" word.

She would stand by the gate looking out at the children playing and I could see she yearned to join them, but would shrink back when they approached with an invitation. They looked, sounded and behaved differently somehow, I could see her thinking, and she wasn't sure what to make of them, if she approved or not. They soon realised we were foreigners

'Muzungu's – Europeans or "Black Muzungu's" as we were known, and their fascination grew. We lived in the suburbs of Nairobi in a fairly new housing development. The local butcher was just across the square in front of the house, on the opposite side of the green where the children played. There was little need for a freezer except to store ice, I bought fresh meat daily and it was just that...fresh. Just a short walk away was an assortment of local kiosks where I could get most things I needed.

My first attempts at speaking Kiswahili brought so much laughter I often resorted to pointing which worked well but did not help me to improve my language skills. However, within a matter of three to four months, our daughter was on her way to fluency and became my interpreter, having been unceremoniously placed outside the gate (locked behind her) and made to engage with the children – what an awful thing to have done. I did keep a close eye on her though and it wasn't long before it was clear she was having a good time, and I left her to it and went indoors. The spectacle of a diminutive child speaking on behalf of her mother greatly amused the local shopkeepers and market traders who would call out to each other demanding that they came to "listen to the child who spoke for the mother" – a rare novelty. I was embarrassed but realised they meant no harm, and soon accepted this would be the norm as, try as I might, I could not grasp the intricacies of the language though I learned to speak it pigeon fashion and could make myself understood with liberal lacings of English.

English and Kiswahili are the official languages of Kenya so living in the capital as we did, I found that most people were conversant with the English language and would immediately switch to English as they realised I was a foreigner. This did not help me to persevere with learning the language, always on the lookout for an easier option.

I was very proud of our daughter's grasp of the languages. By the time she celebrated her fourth birthday she was not only fluent in Kiswahili, she could also greet you and converse pigeon fashion in Kikuyu, Ki-meru and Luo. These were the 'mother tongues' of her friends. Most children, in the city at least, started school speaking at least three languages, being fluent in at least one (the 'mother tongue'). School was taught in English. Kiswahili, as a language, was compulsory. I was informed that parents were brought to task if they were so forgetful of their responsibilities toward their child, as to allow them to start school with no knowledge of the English language. Such children were immediately placed at a disadvantage.

In Kenya it is the custom to have home help, servants called 'house boys' or 'house girls'. Some families had both. We had a young woman from Meru come to live with us hence, our daughter's grasp of that language. I was very proud of her abilities and quite fascinated at how she could switch between the languages throughout conversations quite naturally without a thought, while I was still trying to decipher the first sentence. She spoke KiMeru and Kiswahili to our 'house girl', Kiswahili and English to her dad and *only* English to her brother and me. Kiswahili was the unifying language of choice, with the odd English word thrown into the mix when she was out with her friends.

Her brother did not speak any language other than English, in fact, truth be told, he spoke very little of anything at all and I was quite worried. I tried not to compare his development with that of his sister in recognition of their individuality, but all I had read had led me to believe that second, and subsequent children, often developed at a faster rate as they learned and copied from their siblings. He seemed not to have heard of this theory. When he spoke, it was in English with as few words as possible to make his needs known, then he'd draw on his pipe (his thumb). He'd do this mid sentence as well and often tried to get away with speaking with it still dangling from his lips. On these occasions he'd get no response from me and he'd soon realise why that was. This tactic was adopted after I'd got tired of asking him to remove the offending thumb, and it worked a treat. He was soon cured of his bad habit. Whatever language he was addressed in he responded, appropriately, in English, so I knew he did not lack under-standing and wasn't 'slow' either. He would happily suck his thumb all day and was a very content and happy child. He began kindergar-ten at 2 years and 3months old, so he'd be around other children his age. He loved 'Teacher Rose' who could do no wrong. I cried all the way home from his first day at kinder-garten because he saw his "Teacher Rose" whom he'd been introduced to the previous week, in the distance, ran to her and placed his little hand in hers without even so much as a backward glance for his poor mum. You can imagine how I felt and understand why I was upset. I cried at his sister's first day at school too, but recovered much more quickly as she had turned to wave goodbye.

We returned to England when they were 6 years 9 months and 3 years 5 months respectively, and went to live with my mum for about 5-6 weeks while house hunting. I was relieved we had come home because I had made up my mind to seek advice regarding our son's reluctance to initiate speech except to make his needs known or in response to direct enquiries. Cleary he understood language so what was holding him back? The answer I soon discovered was 'languages', plural. Within 2 weeks of our return, I heard myself saying to him "for goodness sake, can't you be quiet for a moment?" in response to one of his endless demands to tell me something. His little face puckered and I was so full of remorse for snapping at him that I sat him on my knee and asked gently what it was that he wanted to tell me. It was while I was listening with half an ear (I was trying to work out what could have made me snap at my quiet little boy), that I realised that for the past 4-5 days he had not been quiet at all. He had been chatting away about any and everything from the moment he woke until he slept and it had not just been his sister's questions and chatter that I'd had to respond to, but his as well. I just was not used to being in so much demand; it was a shock to my system. I looked at him, and wondered, "What's happened to him?" Then it dawned on me that for the first time in his life, everyone spoke the same language. His confusion, insecurities, whatever it was that had kept him almost trapped in silence was gone. For him, the perfusion of languages was a negative experience. It had held him back. The difference was quite shocking to me and I was so thankful we had not extended our stay in Kenya but had returned home. The seemingly quiet, contented child had become a bubbly, talkative contented child. As young adults, our daughter studied French and our son, Spanish. I continued my efforts with languages and tried coming to terms with the new form of English spoken by some young people where words mean the opposite (not strictly speaking) to what they imply as in if something's 'good', they say it's "bad". Confusing, I know!

The Holy Spirit as Teacher

··•●•··

We all have talents, skills, things we are good at, but often ignore or take for granted, and not put to any useful purpose. Some of them we come across by chance, others we develop by repetition of use or through training, but we all have at least one talent, something we are, or have the potential to be good at, and it is God-given; not randomly, but specifically to fulfil a purpose. We will often miss that purpose if we do not offer those talents back to God, make them available to him, and ask him how to use them.

There are many things that I love to do but am not particularly good at, but could improve with training; and there are many things that I do not love to do but find that I am good at them, even without training, but training would be good.

As a child I loved to sew. When I was about 8 or 9 years old, I made a pleated skirt from a length of green cotton material as part of a school project. I did most of the sewing at home, and all by hand. The pleats I had pinned, tacked, and painstakingly steam pressed in place using one of my dad's handkerchiefs soaked in water and wrung dry; my mum was impressed, and I was proud of my achievement. I was always sewing something, making dolls clothes, pin cushions, hankies, anything really, I even made a hymn book cover for mum's redemption hymnal which, though slightly faded still covers the same well used book today. It had become another of her treasures. When I was 14 years old my dad bought mum a surprise gift, a Singer sewing machine with its own teak storage cupboard with shelves and a drawer. It was kept in their palatial sized bedroom; it was a beautiful piece of furniture and I was desperate to use it. One day I marshalled all my courage and asked her if I could use it expecting a resounding no. I was surprised by her response, coupled with a warning to "take care how I used it". The warning was not against injury to myself, but damage to her treasure, not for what it was, but for who had given it. So began my sewing career.

I began to make my own clothes with the aid of Simplicity and Butterick patterns, and thought I could sew. It wasn't until several years later, married and expecting my first child that I realised I could only follow patterns. I found this out after two attempts to make a maternity dress. I eventually used the fabric as cleaning cloths, that's all it was fit for. I did eventually make two dresses by copying those I'd bought, laying them on the fabric like pattern sheets. When our daughter was born, I tried to make her a few things...how hard could it be? After all, there was no need for things like darts and sophisticated shapes. But those pieces of fabric went the way of their predecessors and became glorified cleaning cloths. I did not give up, and by studying the simple dresses I bought for her, with practice, I soon learned how to make basic children's dresses, dressed up with ribbons, laces and pretty buttons.

So, when we went to Kenya, my plan was to hire a sewing machine and make children's dresses at a reasonable price to supplement our income yet benefit the local people. With this in mind, our daughter became my model and whenever anyone commented on her clothes I would thank them and find a way, without appearing boastful, to mention that I'd made it and would make for their daughters if they desired.

The church we attended ran various training programmes including dressmaking and tailoring, and they loaned me a Singer sewing machine. Unfortunately, it involved learning to use a treadmill and wheel but being blessed with poor hand/feet coordination I could not master the technique and they were kind enough to replace it with an electrical one. It wasn't long before my first customer who wanted a dress made approached me. I was so excited and invited her to visit me at home so I could take measurements. What a shock it was when she arrived, childless, and presented me with a length of material, bought by her husband, and with the express command by the said husband that "no other 'fundi' (seamstress) was to touch the material but me". I was stunned into silence and petrified at the turn of events. Without wanting to disappoint, I carefully explained that I only made children's dresses, had not been trained and was not sure I could fulfil her request. It made not a blind bit of difference. They (her and her husband) believed I could, and her husband was entrusting the task to me. She informed me that there was no difference between making a dress for a child and one for an adult (I could have told her the very obvious differences but felt myself robbed of breath). *And*, she could not take the material to anyone else and would not take it back to her husband. She went on to tell me the material had been specially bought for her in Tanzania by her husband and they had been waiting to have it made up, but did not trust a local 'fundi' with the task. By this time I was ready to lose control of my bladder, excused myself and in the toilet, cried out for help. "What shall I do Lord, you know I can't do this but they are expecting me to. This was not my plan, what shall I do?" There was silence...not a word, and I felt numb. I began a desperate mental search for remembered information from my Simplicity and Butterick sewing past on measurements and how to take them. The only measurements I was sure about was the bust, waist, hip, shoulder to waist and waist to knee/calf ones; darts for shaping bust lines and hips were a mystery to me, where exactly one began and ended. What things to take into consideration, I did not know – and don't even mention collars and cuffs, sleeves, pockets, etc.

I invited her into my sewing room, got a sheet of paper to record her measurements, picked up the tape measure, and all the while I was having a harried conversation with the Holy Spirit. "OK, tell me what I should do...where do I start from? How do I do that...? What about that...?" This was a challenge, God had laid down the gauntlet and I would take it up with his help and so I called on the Holy Spirit continually with every move. Measurements complete, we agreed a fee and she went on her way with confidence while I ran to God with a sense of expectation and trepidation. I knew he could help me, but what if he didn't. *No...don't think that way. He'll help if you trust him...*Yes Lord – I trust you. We'll do this together.

Trusting God did not mean I was anxiety free when it came to drafting a pattern or cutting the material, but I laid it all on Him and kept my eyes on Him throughout the process. I talked through the pattern making with Him, out loud. I wanted to be sure he heard every enquiry. I had 3 metres of fabric to work with, had no idea if it would be enough for the chosen design, and soon learnt that this was the length fabrics were generally sold in (pre-cut), a 'dress length' it was called. When the time came to actually cut the fabric, I prayed, heart pounding in my ears, and then, with pattern pinned to the fabric and scissors poised, I asked the Holy Spirit to go before me and to stop my progress if there was an error in my calculations that would result in my spoiling the fabric. I began to cut, had done several pieces and was about to cut out the bodice when my hand stopped involuntarily and I looked at it and tried to continue but just met a 'pause', that's the only way I can describe it. It would not obey the command of my brain. It was the weirdest thing! I could not see any-thing wrong so asked the Holy Spirit to show me...and He did. I had not made allowances for the darts and this omission would have resulted in the bodice being too small, there was no fabric allowance for errors. He helped me to re-calculate and I used tailors chalk to draw adjustments directly on the fabric. Scis-sor once again poised, I was released to cut until all pieces had been cut out. When it came to sewing the pieces together, the same thing happened, a pause would come over me and I was learning to ask the Holy Spirit to show me where I was going wrong. He always did.

I completed the garment, the fitting went well, she was very pleased and wore the dress to church where her husband thanked me pro-fusely and informed me that all future outfits for his wife would be made by me! The relief and praises I felt couldn't be described...wow. God, the dressmaker...? Why not.

That was the end of my dream to make chil-dren's clothing (except for my own kids) and the beginning of my adventures with women's clothing. The orders came hard and fast. I tried in vain to refuse some when I could not see how it was humanly possible to complete them all, but no one would take no for an answer, everyone was willing to wait for however long it took. I actually had a waiting list and some waited almost a year, happily, because "they knew I would do a good job". I had no such confidence in myself but had rapidly developed every confidence in the Holy Spirit my private tutor. I heard myself agreeing to designs I had absolutely no idea how to execute, drawing designs as though the sewing of it would be the easiest thing in the world, all with a sense of unreality and wonder. My Teacher stood by me all the way, taught me things I did not know and would never have guessed. I made A-line dresses, flared dresses, pleated dresses (all done by hand until I discovered I could send the fabric to be pleated at a reasonable price), suits (skirts and tops) and bridesmaid satin/lace fancy dresses. I even made matching belts and covered buttons.

I made toilet bags and sold them to a local pharmacy, and frilled bedspreads, after the Austrian blinds style. That was a hit. I sold several privately.

It was amazing the things I found I could do under His tutelage. It was exciting and frightening, but all very practical and helpful for all concerned. It paid our bills and saved them money while they received good quality, well made products. I loved to sew, but my skills were in their infancy until I received training from on high. I also had some help from a book on metric pattern cutting that my husband bought for me on a trip home. A lot of the information was incomprehensible to me and required divine interpretation. I even progressed to making my sons PJs and trousers, and a pair of tailored shorts for my husband (that was once we had returned home, and I was shocked at their prices in the shops). Throughout those years, and even today, I can never sew a thing without first consulting my Teacher. That pause still comes over me and I know there is something that I have not considered; He always points it out to me and guides me through the process. I depend on Him to.

Did you know that the Holy Spirit is an excellent cake decorator and florist too? I discovered this one morning after church when mingling amongst the congregation of a few hundred. A young man approached me with an invitation to his wedding. I was surprised and touched because we had only been in Kenya for about 5 months, and he was really keen for us to share his day with him. He asked if I would make his wedding cake. He simply assumed that I could make wedding cakes, and to my shock and horror, I heard myself say that "he would have the best wedding cake ever" and it would be our gift to him and his bride. I could not believe it, what was I saying? Where did those words come from? They had certainly not formulated in my mind or I would have interrupted them, they just fell from my tongue. What on earth was I going to do? "Lord, what shall I do?" *Keep your word*. I did, and it was amazing, I was amazed, the bride and groom were amazed, their guests were amazed, and the orders came flooding in. I learned sugar craft and made all sorts of intricate designs from icing sugar. I learnt how to be innovative with limited resources and continually amazed myself. I'd stand back and look at the end results and wonder how I could have done it. The answer was always the same, 'with God's help'. I concluded that there was nothing He could not do; He'd said it and I was proving it to be absolutely true. All we have to do is to put our talents, abilities and skills in His hands and wait to see what He will do with them. After all, He gave them to us so He is sure to have a purpose for them. I went to Kenya as a wife and mother. I did not preach, or teach, lead a lady's group or anything usually expected of a missionary's wife. I did not fit the bill in that respect, and at times had felt embarrassed when saying no to the many requests for me to do such things. But God made room for what I could do, and it blessed my family and me, and those we served. He taught me to accept my limitations, to be comfortable in my own skin and not to try and fit into one of someone else's making, to put all my talents in His hands and allow Him to use them for His purpose. I try to do this always, and I have also learnt that when He challenges me, it's because He knows what He has placed within me, and is providing me with an opportunity to find, recognise and use it.

To obey is better than Sacrifice

··•●•··

My husband was actively involved with a local church, teaching and training leaders in the capacity of a missionary. I kept home and raised our young family; our daughter was 5 years old, our son 18+ months old. I'd made several friends from amongst the congregation and regularly made and received social calls. God began to work in me in a new way, through word of knowledge and visions with startling results. I was always slow to respond to His urging because it brought unwanted attention to me and I much preferred to blend into the background. I was about to learn obedience on a different level, to learn that it was not about me, but about Him and what he wanted to do in His children's lives through me and those who were willing to be used.

I had recently begun to attend 'Women Aglow' meetings and was beginning to understand how much God loved me and would not allow me to hold on to things that were damaging to me, such as un-forgiveness, however justified my actions may seem. To forgive was a command. At one meeting I was praying for a refreshing of the Holy Spirit when He informed me that un-forgiveness was a barrier to His infilling. I was surprised as I was not aware of its' presence in my life. So, I asked him to show me; He went on to reveal a time when I had been hurt repeatedly by the same person and of the secret promise I had made to myself never to forgive their hurt. I had forgotten that promise, but once out in the light I was convicted of my error and sought forgiveness. I was then told to seek the forgiveness of this person and I did, in writing, as we were continents apart. I received a written response also asking for forgiveness. We became very close. One thing God had asked of me having refreshed my spirit; was that I wait on him early in the mornings and that I worshipped and listened.

One morning during my time with him I had a vision. I was standing by my bedroom window looking out across the square and saw a friend approaching. I noted that she was wearing a suit I had made for her. I also noted all that was taking place in the square, the open butcher shop with customers waiting to be served, the children playing – I recognised most of them as my neighbour's children, and the sound of dogs barking. She crossed the square and knocked on the main security gate. At that moment God spoke to me and said I should not let her leave until I had prayed for her. The vision ended and I asked God what was happening. I thought I'd fallen asleep on my knees so I continued to pray for a while, then got up and began my daily routine but I could not get the image of my friend out of my mind. Later that morning having completed the ironing, I took a pile of clothes up to my bedroom to put away. The last few pieces in hand, I walked across the room to the wardrobe situated beside the window and put the clothes on the shelf. As I closed the door and turned to leave the room, I glanced out the window and froze. There, coming across the square was my friend wearing the suit I had made for her as I had seen in the vision. It was like action replay as I glanced around the square at the various activities taking place. I could not move. I began to mutter, "Oh my God, oh my God". I thought, what is God doing? What shall I do? Oh my God!

I ran downstairs to let her in. I smiled and chatted but all the time my stomach vacillated between churning and knots and my mind screamed, "oh my God what shall I do?" Of course, I knew the answer, but tried to reject it. We chatted and had 'Chai' (tea) for a few hours before she rose to leave. All this while the Holy Spirit was reminding me of what I should do, but I didn't know how. I had never prayed for anyone before in such a situation and in this way. What do I do, just say can I pray for you and pray? What if she thought I was weird or something? I was a housewife and mother, that's all. She seemed OK to me.

She went out the door and I followed her to the gate. She took one step through the gate, and the Holy Spirit almost screamed it seemed with urgency *"Don't let her leave until you've prayed for her"* He was so forceful I nearly jumped. My right arm shot out and caught her arm to pull her back through the gate. I asked her if I could pray for her. I explained that I felt it was what God wanted me to do. She agreed and came back into the house. She wanted to know if she should sit, stand or kneel. I stared at her hoping she couldn't see my nervousness and said, "Whatever you want". She knelt and I thought, oh God, now what? He said *"Pray."* I thought, *"pray what?"* I had no idea what to say but I raised my hand over her head and hoped God would give me the words. I said, *"oh God"* and got no further. She collapsed on the floor like she had been struck. I stepped back staring and asking God what was happening. I didn't know what to do or say next. "Pray" He repeated, so I prayed something like this, "Oh God, you created your child and You know all about her. You know her needs and her troubles. I ask You to touch her and bring healing from the crown of her head to the soles of her feet." I remember passing my hand from the top of her head to her feet. I sat back on my hunches and watched and waited. Half an hour passed with no change. What do I do Lord? "Wait" He replied. I waited, and then noticed tears flowing down the side of her face into her ear, filling the little channel and overflowing into her hairline. She stirred and sat up and I helped her onto the sofa and gave her some tissues. She looked at me and smiled after a long while, and then thanked me for praying for her.

Without going into great detail, she told me that that morning she had seen her husband off to work, had taken her children to school and felt she needed to tell me goodbye. She saw my confusion, "Goodbye? Where are you going" It was then I learned that her plan had been to leave me and go to the river. I knew the one she meant, the bodies of those who had taken their lives were found in that river

almost daily. Some were never found. She had
been desperate and without hope. Her life had
seemed unbearable and she was going to end
it, had been on her way but felt she needed to
see me, to say "goodbye", so had made a detour
to my home. I had been God's chosen lifeline to
his hurting child. I, with all my timidity, insecurities, doubts, and endless questions, had
been His choice. We hugged and cried together
and all the while I was thinking that if I had
not obeyed God at the last minute, she would
have died and I would have had to bear that
responsibility. I can still feel the sense of
dread that came over me at the realisation of
how high the price of disobedience could be.
God had chosen weak, timid, shy, fearful me to
be a lifeline to one of His drowning children. I
prayed there and then, "Lord, please never let
any of these weaknesses prevent me from doing your will." The cost is too great.

At these times in my life, I hold on to the
knowledge that Gods' strength is perfected in
our weaknesses, and that to obey is always
better than sacrifice. Am I any bolder today?
No, not really. More obedient? Yes, but there
is still room for improvement; I trust in his
grace and strive to be Christ like daily.

Storm in a teacup

···•●•···

It is always best to stay on the right side of the
law, but sometimes in spite of our best efforts
the enemy has some evil plan to upset the ap-
ple cart. It is good to know that God sees,
knows, and can do all things. On this occasion,
my husband acting on behalf of the church
Elder, had placed his signature on documents
which, due to miscommunication meant that
he was responsible for payment of a large sum
of money to a hotel that had housed foreign
guests of the church. The situation could not
be resolved until the person who had made the
agreement by phone was available. They were
abroad on business but expected back any day.
However, the hotel was pressing for payment
and threatening to involve the police. We certainly did not have the kind of money they
demanded. Things were looking very bleak
and we prayed for God to intervene and make
a way for my husband who was at the centre
of it, due to his signature, and that everything
would be settled to the hotel and guests' satisfaction.

Life continued as usual and on this particular Saturday we were to attend a wedding at the church. My husband was highly stressed by the dark cloud that was overshadowing him with the awful implications for himself and his family if he were arrested before the Elder returned, due later that day. We prayed before we left home. We could do no more. The stress was causing him to experience tightening of the chest and he was having difficulty breathing. I was worried for his health and continued to pray for him as we drove to the church. He would not take my advice to not attend the wedding, nor did he follow my advice to take a taxi and not drive.

We arrived early so I went to pass the time with a friend who lived in an apartment just across the road while he went on to the church office. She had just finished baking a batch of cakes and offered me a slice with a cup of tea, which I accepted with thanks. We chatted as she prepared it. She first brought me a slice of cake, and then the tea served in a fine bone china cup and saucer. As I raised the cup to my lips, watching the tea ripple and shimmer as I did so, I had a vision – *I saw my husband walking toward the church, shoulders drooping, face drawn and dejected looking. I ran to him and he put his arm about my shoulder and I bore his weight as we walked toward the church. I felt surprise that he embraced me in this way publicly because we were always careful not to offend anyone by behaving in a culturally unacceptable way. The opposite sexes did not display extended physical contact in public. I enquired, "What was the matter?" To which, he responded that he'd tell me in his office (at the church). Arriving there, he sat on the chair behind his desk hardly able to speak, gasping, words coming singly, separated by great rasps of breath...he was consumed with worry. I had never seen him in such a state and with the laying-on of hands; I began to pray for him, but was interrupted by a knock at the door. Three times I was interrupted before I finally succeeded in praying for him –* the cup was inches from my lips and I was staring at the ripples as they caught the light. Elsie was still speaking to me but I had no idea what she had said. I felt an overwhelming sense of urgency and stood as I put the cup back in the saucer and on the table, said I had to go, promised to return, and headed for the door explaining that my husband needed me. I didn't wait for a response and didn't stop to wonder what she thought of my words or actions, I just ran...down five flights of stairs, taking the last two or three in each flight at a jump. I ran around the side of the building to the road and as I waited to cross over I looked toward the church and there was my husband as God had shown me.

All that followed was as I had seen it to the smallest detail, every word, every action, and every interruption. And as it unfolded, I watched and participated in amazement as though I were living through a dream. It was the strangest feeling.

I did not wait to see what results my prayers would bring, there could only be one, relief, after all, God was at work. The fact that He chose to use me was not significant. He could have used anyone. Ultimately all He needed was someone who would be obedient. I went back to my friend and had my tea and cake.

Later my husband told me he didn't know what would have happened if I had not prayed. His chest had been tight and painful and he'd had difficulty breathing. God had shown me the storm brewing in a teacup and as Jesus spoke to the waves and calmed the sea, so He spoke into the situation and brought calm, but it was not over. The following day it flared up again and his condition was even worse to the point that he would have ran over a pedestrian if I had not cried out and brought his attention back to the road and driving. His mind was pre-occupied and even after this near miss he insisted on continuing the journey because he needed to update the Elder who had returned late the previous night. His breathing was laboured, his vision clouded with worry and as I looked at the children and 'house girl' (home help) sitting in the back I prayed continuously in 'tongues' until we arrived at the church.

Arriving there he went directly to the Elder's office to update him on events while I went into the Church (a supersize tent) with the children to settle for morning praise and worship. As people arrived and settled in seats about me, I continued to pray. God spoke to me then by His Holy Spirit and commanded me to go and pray for my husband. I wondered how I was going to interrupt the Elder's interview with him and delayed. More urgently the command "go and pray for your husband" came. Remembering what would have been the result of disobedience the last time God had spoken so insistently, I leaped from my seat, thrusting our son (a toddler) in my neighbours lap as I did so and asking her to watch him and our daughter. Running to the office I knocked and entered without waiting for a response. I could not believe my boldness. I stated that I "needed to pray for my husband" who was slouching forward in his chair before the Elder clutching at his chest. I laid my hand on him and prayed. I didn't know what to pray but that didn't matter, God knew. Apologising for disturbing them I went back to the children and waited. Before long they both came in with the other leaders. He looked free of worry and was smiling. We had a great time that morning praising God. Everything was handed over and later resolved and my husband delivered. God doesn't always require us to understand our actions, only to be willing to trust Him and obey His word.

Not mine, but yours

··•◉•··

We had returned to the UK for almost a year, our son was now four and a half years old, and had joined his sister at school. He began on a Thursday completing two half days, 9-12noon. This was followed on Monday with a full day and so it should have continued, but on Monday afternoon when I met them in the playground after school, he was very quiet and looked poorly. He had a temperature and refused his dinner so he had a glass of warm milk and an early night. I had given him 5mls of Calpol before he went to bed and checked on him at about 10.30p.m. when we retired ourselves. He was still quite hot, and I stayed up to give him another dose for the night. Finally, I was able to get some sleep myself. He still had a temperature in the morning, so I contacted the child minder to request that she kept him for the day. I had started a new job two weeks previously, and was still on the probationary period so did not want to take any time off unnecessarily. I thought it might be another of those 24hr bugs that children are so prone to. He had certainly had his fair share in the past. I wasn't unduly worried, so I packed his bag for the day including the bottle of Calpol and written instructions and our contact numbers.

When I picked him up after work he seemed about the same, had lost his appetite completely and had only sips of drinks. This was also true to his usual pattern and he always made up for lost opportunities once recovered, so I didn't press him. I continued with the Calpol and again he had an early night. At about 2a.m. we woke to the sound of a loud banging and leaped out of bed falling over each other in our hurry to get to the door. Once in the hallway we realised the sound came from our sons' room and ran in to find him convulsing on his bed with such force the bed was banging against the wall.

I sent my husband to call the doctor while I put the pillow and quilt between our son and the wall and sat on the edge of his bed to prevent his falling off. I spoke to him calmly and clearly so he would know I was there and not be afraid. I did my best to comfort him. Eventually, I was able to place a thermometer under his arm and get a fan on him by which time the doctor arrived – the surgery was about eight doors down the road. His temperature was 103C and she prescribed 10mls Calpol 4hrly, and tepid baths to lower his temperature. She explained that the seizure had been the result of his high temperature. She called again at 9.00a.m. Wednesday morning to check his progress. His temperature had fallen to 102C, and she advised increasing the calpol to 15mls 4hrly and to sponge him down with cool water and offer lots to drink. I stayed home with him carrying out the doctors' instructions, although I had some reservations about the increased dose as it contradicted the recommendations on the instruction leaflet. I chose to keep the dose at 10mls. He would tolerate sips of water only but seemed to lose twice as much as he took in immediately after when he vomited which weakened him so I only gave him enough to wet his dry mouth.

When the combination of Calpol, sponging and a fan did not get his temperature down I rang the surgery. By now it was about 6.45pm and the doctor on call came out and advised I continue as I was. This I refused to do. My son had not eaten and barely drunk anything since Monday evening. His temperature wavered between 101-102C and he was very weak. I insisted on an ambulance being called to get him to the hospital. While waiting, I got his sister into her pyjamas with a track suit on top, packed a bag with books, toys and a snack for her and another bag with pyjamas and bits for her brother. I didn't think about myself, I was racing against the clock, expecting the ambulance to arrive at any time. I tried to contact their father and was unable to. He had left the office for a meeting so I left him a note explaining what was happening and asking him to come to the hospital to collect our daughter as soon as possible.

He arrived on the ward at about 11p.m., our daughter was asleep on a chair. There was nothing further I could tell him of our son's illness. He had been examined twice and no one seemed to know what was wrong with him, so his care plan was no different. I was still offering sips of water and sponging him down. He had a drip set up as he was dehydrated. When eventually my husband left with our daughter, I informed him that he would have to make arrangements for her for school and informed him where to find the various numbers for the childminder and friends who would offer support. I knew I could not leave the hospital.

I had been praying and asking God to touch and heal our son since Monday evening. I continued to pray, sometimes in 'tongues', asking God to reveal to the various doctors what was wrong with him so they could prescribe the right treatment, or to just heal him outright. I suspected that he had meningitis but apart from the high temperature there was no other indication. The doctors checked for a rash and regularly manipulated his head and limbs for the classic signs of stiffening to no avail, all were very supple. Deep down I was convinced he had meningitis and from their examination it seemed that this was what they suspected too. I prayed fervently, "Lord, please heal my son" over and over again. This had been my prayer since Tuesday night.

By Thursday morning he was listless and it seemed almost lifeless. When I called his name he tried to move his head in the direction of my voice but did not seem to have the strength or the ability to focus. Eventually he could not even open his eyes. When I lifted his hand off the bed and released it, it just fell back, lifeless, it seemed upon the sheet. When I held his hand, he could not hold mine, He had no strength to. I looked at my son and he appeared to be slipping away from me. Throughout the night three paediatricians had examined him and all they could say was "this is very strange". I felt like screaming. If they did not know what was wrong, if they could not help him, whom could I look to but God? When my husband rang to check on his progress before leaving for work that morning, I had no news for him.

I was now physically and emotionally exhausted. I had not slept since Tuesday night when his convulsions woke us up. I knew not what else to pray except "Lord, heal my son." It took over my mind and I could hardly speak or think of anything else. I looked at the big clock on the wall; it was 10 o'clock on Thursday morning. I was drained, hungry and in need of a wash and change of clothing. I needed to do something, but what? I couldn't sit there watching anymore, and I could not pray anymore, not because I'd given up, but because I'd run out of what to say to effect the change I desired. I needed to get home to freshen up and I needed to make further arrangements for our daughter. I decided that I would pray just once more before leaving for a quick trip home to freshen up. I looked about me and there was nowhere private so I went into the toilet, paused for a while, then told God what my son meant to me. I described him as though God had never seen him before and asked, "Please heal my son." Suddenly, God revealed his displeasure at my stating that Richard was "my son" as though he were solely mine, not even his father's claim was acknowledged. He was not just my son; he was God's son too; first even. God had 'gifted' him to me. None of us are our own; we all belonged to God. I apologised for my selfish prayer and thanked God for blessing us with a son. I thanked Him for the love and joy He brought into our lives, then, I offered him back to God. I said, "if you want your child back, please take him and give me the strength to bear it, but if you want me to continue to nurture him to manhood, then please reveal to the doctors what is wrong with him and use them to heal him or perform a miracle of healing." I could not imagine how I would continue without him, but I trusted God to give me the strength if that was his decision. I told the nurse I was going home and would return ASAP.

I was gone for one and three quarter hours exactly. On the bus journey home I purposely focussed my thoughts on our daughter and her immediate needs and how best I could arrange for them to be met without loss of time. I then considered my husbands' schedule for the next few days and how he fitted into the arrangements for our daughter so that life remained as near to normal as possible for her. Then on myself and work arrangements for time off. I also planned how I would live between the hospital and home for the next few days at least. The return journey to the hospital was much more difficult. My mind kept wandering back to our son so to avoid the temptation of negative thoughts, I went on a trip down memory lane to his birth and life since and struggled between tears and laughter and somehow manage to keep thoughts of the hospital at bay.

When I eventually walked onto the ward my heart was pounding, I could hear the heavy *thud* of it echoing in my ears and I felt sick with apprehension. What would God decide? Whatever it was could only be right. He is God. I girded my loins, so to speak, took a deep painful breath and rounded the corner to my son's bed hoping but ready for whatever would meet my eyes. He was sitting up in bed! He looked up at me, "Hi mum," he said smiling at me with a toy in his hand and telling me about what the doctors had done to him and more, just as though it was perfectly normal to be on a hospital ward. He began to tell me about the playroom, the other children, his friend...and I just sat on the end of his bed and stared at him. I wanted to hug him but couldn't because he was behaving in such a natural, normal way that I felt he would not understand my excitement and emotion and it might scare him. Words failed me. How could I thank God? What could I say? Words were surely inadequate to express the joy that was a tangible pain in my chest. My head felt light as I strove to take in the enormity of what I was witnessing. I had offered God His son and He had given him back to me. He had given him back to me, whole. That's how much He loved me. His words *try me and prove me, with me you are safe* rang in my ear. He cannot lie. He had kept His promise to me again.

The consultant paediatrician and nurse were with him and explained that shortly after I'd left the hospital, they had examined him again and his neck was fixed indicating meningitis. This had necessitated the removal of spinal fluid to determine the strain and appropriate treatment. He had received the first course of antibiotics, and in their own words, they "couldn't understand it. His recovery was so immediate that if they did not have the evidence of their own eyes and his test results, they would send him home, but, as it was, he would have to spend the full recovery time on the ward" (13 days in all). I had no such difficulty. One word, God.

That very evening he had sausages, chips and beans for tea. By the next day he was running about and was unstoppable. He soon became bored with the restrictions placed on the supposedly 'sick' child. On discharge I was told he would need a sight, hearing and I think, language test to check for any damage resulting from the illness. I took the appointment cards but knew it was a waste of time. I had asked God to take him or heal him. I did not expect anything less. I got nothing less. Six weeks later he was given a clean bill of health. If, at fifteen, he had seemed not always to have heard what was said, I put it down to the selective hearing that often troubled teenagers.

Sometimes we forget that the whole world and all that's in it was made by and for God. We claim it as our own and do not acknowledge the giver's rights. God has blessed me with a family, a home and many possessions. I hold onto them with a loose hand realising that at any moment they can be taken. They are temporal however lovely, however desirable. But my salvation I hold fast to by the grace of God.

It is my most valuable possession and by whatever means the enemy may use to attack, his ultimate goal is to trick me into letting go of my salvation and hold onto temporal, passing treasures. God says we should not store up treasures here on earth but to seek that which is eternal and imperishable.

God of the impossible

···•●•···

To say something is impossible to a Christian is like holding a red flag to a bull, it becomes a challenge to their faith, one to which they rise because it is really a 'win win' situation.

When we returned from Kenya, we went to live in London with my mother temporarily. That was the base from which we found jobs and a home. Both were accomplished within two months. I was shocked to discover how the cost of living had rocketed in the four years we were abroad, and the price we'd have to pay to rent a home. Three bedroomed houses or flats in London were either beyond our means, or in a totally unsuitable location for a family with young children who had known nothing but suburban life, clean air and open safe play areas. Eventually we decided to look further afield and Orpington caught my eye. It brought back memories of my early adult life when I'd pass through Orpington station on my way to work in Tunbridge Wells. I had loved the name and had always imagined it to be a nice place. It was, and the rental price for housing was reasonable when compared to

London with much preferable location for the children.

After two years in Orpington, during which time we had had a rent increase and were now faced with the notification of a third increase that would consume, very nearly, my whole month salary, I suggested to my husband that we bought our own home. The mortgage would be less than the rent we were paying-even without the increase, and it would be an investment for the future. Those were the days when it really was a viable investment. Though at first reluctant, he saw that it made good sense and we were able to raise a mortgage of £53,000. It was nowhere near enough but it would have to do. I went to all the estate agents on the high street and told them what we wanted, which was a 4-bedroom house with bathroom/toilet, and an additional toilet. I had already calculated our needs specifically. The fourth bedroom was to accommodate an au pair for the children, and the extra toilet to accommodate their synchronised bodily functions. I had had enough of deciding who needed the bathroom most urgently and had told God so. I was very specific in my request to Him, giving details of my reasons behind each specification. The fourth bedroom for the Au pair would accommodate my work duties. As a carer I worked shifts, early mornings, late evenings and nights. It was becoming increasingly difficult and costly to arrange childcare to suit all our needs. This seemed like a sensible option and, thank God, it worked out well.

I did not think I was being extravagant. I had just assessed my family's basic needs. This was the minimum I could accept and told God about it, asking Him to provide. We had four to five months notice before the beginning of the new rental agreement so I asked God to provide before our present contract expired. This was before we had arranged a mortgage so I was a little concerned that we could borrow such a small amount. However, armed with a mortgage, God's promise for my life, and the knowledge that figures were immaterial to Him, I went house hunting. You can imagine my feelings when one after the other, all the estate agents told me it was impossible to get a four bedroomed house with bathroom and additional toilet for £53,000. They suggested that we might be lucky and get a two bedroomed flat, but that a one bedroomed maisonette or starter home was more likely. Well...I didn't believe in luck I believed in God and repeated our requirements so they could take down the details. They promised to send us information on anything that came up and they did, for one and two bedroomed properties. I dumped them all, rang the offices and repeated our requirements. On a few occasions they sent us information on three bedroomed properties but I dumped them too. If it did not state four bedrooms, it did not get read. What was the point? It was not what I'd asked God for. It is interesting to note that even those rejected properties were several thousand pounds above the mortgage we had been given.

When about four weeks had passed without any further contact, I went to each office to check on their progress and to remind them in person of our very specific needs and also that we were open to view repossessed properties. By this time, I'm sure they thought I'd lost the plot. Impossible seemed to be a word they reserved for me, but not one I recognised in connection with God. I let another month go by never doubting God would provide. I was very comfortable with that knowledge. It was time for another visit as we were running out of time. I always started at the same end of the high street, worked my way down one side and up the other before catching the bus home. I examined the window display of the first office before stepping in. The expression on their faces changed, but I ignored it and waited. They were all waiting for the other to attend to me and I just looked from one to the other wondering which it would be, who would be brave enough. It became an embarrassingly long wait when they were obviously not busy, I being their only customer, embarrassing for them. I had all the time in the world and made that clear – secretly I empathised with them, they could not see where I was coming from. Eventually a young lady approached apologising for keeping me waiting. I repeated my details and asked if anything new had come in. She gave me the latest information which had nothing suitable, apologised and promised to keep looking, and began to walk me to the door when one of her colleagues, a young man, asked if the property in St Paul's Cray had gone. She looked puzzled at first then said she didn't think it was suitable. I asked why? She then said it was an ex-council house in need of total cleaning and redecoration and had been on the market for some time. Squatters and their dogs had moved in and wrecked it. It had been on the market for some time and had just arrived at their office. The asking price was £59,995. It had been repossessed hence the price. It was open plan on the ground floor, with four bedrooms, bathroom/toilet and downstairs closet. It was our house.

I arranged a viewing for the following day and arrived early so I could look around the area first. An elderly man came out of his house and told me if I had come to view the house he would advise against it. "It's not a nice area," he said. I thanked him and waited but I considered his words and thought, my God has answered my very specific prayer, He has also promised that I would be safe with Him. Who was I to believe? God or man? I already had my answer. The agent had understated the condition of the property but it was not beyond redemption and I was excited as I watched God at work. I arranged another visit for my husband to see it too. He was unsure because of its location and condition and left the decision to me. I had no concerns that God could not deal with, the first being the price.

We wrangled backward and forward over this for a few weeks. I knew I was bargaining from a position of strength on both counts, it was the house God had chosen, and it had been on the market for nearly eighteen months with various agents with few offers. I started at

£48,000 because of the amount of work needing to be done, they responded with £59,000. I increased my offer to £50,000, they responded with £57,500. I then offered £52,000 and they responded with £55,000 minimum. I gave it a few days thought, talking through with God all the way, always confident that an agreement would be made but hoping to keep some of the money for the repairs. I made a last offer of £53,000 and after a week they came back with a figure of £53,500. We accepted this, raised the £500.00 and signed the contract. We arranged a small loan to complete the repairs, cleaning and decorating with the help of a family friend and his work team, and brothers and sisters in the Lord who donated various pieces of furniture.

We were able to extend our rented accommodation contract by one month. This allowed us time to carryout necessary repairs. The estate agent had provided us with a set of keys to the property for the work to be done before we had signed contracts and they received payment. This was all in answer to our prayers as we could not afford to pay a mortgage and rent in the same month.

Over the years we have had no more than the normal level of trouble or irritation of noisy or rude neighbours. In general, it has been a pleasant place to live and I have few regrets. Having two toilets did not solve the problem. Children can be very perverse. They always seemed to want the one that was in use. I gave up attempting to sort out that problem. We used Au pairs for childcare for 4 years. We had short-term (1-2wks) foreign students for a few years. Our home was never empty. The fourth bedroom has housed Au pairs, students of different nationalities, sisters in Christ needing temporary accommodation, and friends from overseas. It has been an office, a games room and a general 'don't know where to store it' odds and sods room.

I was told *impossible* by five estate agents but even if a thousand had said the same, would that diminish Gods power or reduce His provision in any way? Of course not. I had prayed and had an assurance that God would answer. When we limit ourselves to the physical, what we can see and touch through lack of faith, we can only do and achieve so much because we limit God. But when we free ourselves spiritually and let our faith rise, nothing is impossible.

Trust

From time to time we all fall into the error of depending on ourselves and on our own efforts. At least I'd like to think I'm not the only one. When this happens, we get frantic and stressed until we realise the cause and transfer our dependency back to God.

When my husband gave up his job to go to university full-time, I knew it would be tough. He had been the main breadwinner. How could we possibly manage without his salary? We revised our expenditure, did away with the frills, and I prepared in every way I could for the time ahead. I got a second job and concentrated on paying the bills.

Things were as hard as I had expected, and at times worse. I struggled with the responsibilities of the home and family while he lived away from home, returning once or twice a month only. I was constantly doing a balancing act to keep our heads above water. The more the bills came in and the pressure built up, the harder and longer I worked to get the money in, and the less I depended on God. Even though I was praying every day, I had stopped listening. When God told me not to worry, I worked harder. A two job juggle, became three – I just was not listening. How could God get and hold my attention long enough to effect a change?

He used a dumb animal, and it's not the first time either; remember Naaman and his ass? He used our cat Benji. It was 8.15a.m. and I'd been at work for forty-five minutes when the phone rang and I was told my son was on the line and he sounded upset. That was an understatement. He was hysterical and sobbing so much his speech was unintelligible. I could not understand a word he said and I felt faint with dread. I imagined something had happened to his sister. I raised my voice and spoke firmly asking him to slow down, to take a deep breath and start again. I felt cruel because he was clearly in shock but I needed to know what had happened and I needed to know quickly before I lost it myself. In the midst of all the babble I got two words "Benji" and "car" and a wave of relief swept over me. His sister was OK. This was rapidly followed by fear for him; he was clearly in shock and needed help. Unravelling his jumbled words, I gathered that a car had struck Benji and he had witnessed it. Benji was crying and unable to move lying in the middle of the road and it was his fault because Benji had been following him to school, and he had shooed him away so the cat had run across the road and was hit by a passing car. The driver did not stop and he didn't know what to do.

I directed him to go to our neighbour and tell her what had happened and she would take care of everything until I got there. I left work immediately and prayed all the way, for my son and Benji, he was our daughter's cat and she would be upset. I got home and reassured and calmed our son, got Benji into the car and the three of us rushed to the veterinary surgery. He was found to have a suspected broken pelvis requiring an x-ray to confirm and an operation followed by rest at the practice for a few days. I thought "Oh God. How will I pay the bill? Only the previous day I had checked our account and found we had £3.72 in it, I also had £20 in my purse. The bill was estimated to be in excess of £200 and my mind went blank. This was one problem/bill too much. I already had red letters for the gas and electricity bills, other bills were due soon. What would I do? I was praying but not believing. When asked if I could afford the bill, I said I would have to but it would be difficult.

The Vet agreed to my paying with post-dated cheques of £50 a month to cover the cost.

I spent the rest of the day worrying about the bill and shared my difficulty with my neighbour and sister in Christ. That night after the children had gone to bed I went to my room, got on my knees and asked God "why?" I reminded him of our financial situation as though He didn't know; and wondered why, since he could have prevented it, had He not? "Why didn't you?" I cried. And very clearly, He said, "so that you learn to trust me. So that you understand that when I say ask and it shall be given, that is what I mean." And into my mind came the scripture "ask and it shall be given unto you, seek and you shall find, knock and it shall be opened unto you". So, I prayed "Father, I am seeking your help, I'm knocking at your door and asking that you provide the finance I need for Benji's bill." – (words to that effect and more besides) but at the end of it, I felt a sense of calm and waiting.

Two days later when I went to collect Benji from the surgery and asked for the bill, I was told his treatment amounted to £55.75 so I asked for the whole bill, the complete amount. The receptionist looked at the computer screen and repeated the amount. I said "yes, that's the first instalment but what of the balance?" She looked at me confused as I repeated that what she'd quoted was an instalment only. I looked at her puzzled as to why it was not clear to her what the Vet had agreed just two days previously; it should be on Benji's record. I was asked to wait while she consulted with the Vet and a few minutes later he came out of his surgery and confirmed my bill of £55.75. He said he had not charged me for the Xray (£80), the operation or for the time Benji spent at the practice. I was only charged for the drugs used which had to be replaced. I could not believe my ears. Yet my heart said "why not?" God had said I should trust him; that I should ask (trusting) if I wanted to receive. I wrote a cheque for the full amount (post dated) thanked him and left. I thanked God all the way home and also asked Him to bless the surgeon and his practice. A lesson learnt and forgotten, not practiced, was taught again. God had answered my prayer and provided. He could be trusted to keep His word.

When I arrived home with Benji, the mail was waiting on the coffee table with a note to call a couple from our church also. I opened the mail first and there was a Banker's Draft for £200, written on the back were the words "with love", no name no note, nothing. Who had sent this? I could hardly believe my eyes. God had provided more than enough for Benji. I then rang the couple and spoke to the wife who informed me that they had heard about Benji and felt God wanted them to pay the bill that they'd heard would be in excess of £200. I thanked her, chatted a bit and hung up the phone. I was stunned at their offer and my eyes fell on the cheque lying on the table before me. I rang her back to thank them again and to explain that I had received a cheque that more than covered the cost of the bill as this had been greatly reduced. I explained what the Vet had done for me, thanked her again for their offer and hung up.

A few minutes later she was on the phone to me. She had reported everything to her husband and they still felt they should obey God and pay the bill and they would drop a cheque round later that evening. I thanked her a third time, hung up the phone and sat staring at it for some time. I looked around the room, at the children; all seemed normal, and then back at the phone and the cheque. Was this really happening? Yes, it was. I'd thought the miracle of God's provision at the surgery wonderful. It was enough for me but not for God. An hour later I received the cheque for £55 that would clear in my account before my post-dated cheque would be called on. I had paid a massive 75p in total for Benji's treatment. I still had £200 on my hands and asked God what I should do with it. He reminded me of the gas and electricity bills awaiting settlement; I had hidden them away, out of sight out of mind had become my strategy for coping when overwhelmed with bills. Together they amounted to £198.73 (approx.). I rang the company to inform them that the payment would not reach their account before the cut off date stated in their red letter, they agreed not to cut off my power source.

There I was running back and forth like a headless chicken, working and worrying myself to a bone when if I'd only listened and practised what I had been taught and knew, I would have saved myself the bother. It took a dumb animal (and I don't mean dumb in a negative or derogatory way) to get my attention and a merciful Father to forgive my presumption. "Come unto me and I will give you rest, take my yoke upon you and learn of me for I am meek and lowly."

Lesson learnt, I put it into practice and prayed through and listened/waited through every need and they were all met, some miraculously. I cannot say why having trusted God before, I had ceased to do so on this occasion. I can only thank God that He did not leave me in that state because He loves me.

The writing is on the wall

··•●•··

I am still learning that when I can't, God can. I remember when my daughter was at primary school that she needed help to write a poem, and came to me. I panicked because naturally she expected a 'grown up' would be able to offer the support she needed. The truth was that as a child I had never been able to write or understand poetry. I liked rhyming verse even though I did not always understand it. In the end I had to confess that poetry was not my favourite subject and maybe her father would be of more help. After a few attempts, she probably agreed.

I had always wanted to write and felt sure that one day I would publish a book, but it wouldn't be a book of poetry. Oh no, not poetry. That is until the day I was admitted to hospital for a minor operation. Within a few hours I was bored and had read a magazine from front to back, something I had never done before and hope never to again. What was I to do over the next few days? It had been an emergency admission so I was unprepared for the tedium of the long days with nothing to do.

For reasons that will become clear later, I was at the lowest point in my life that I could remember. Nothing had ever come near this. I felt alone, but for God, and distraught; a hospital ward was the last place I wanted to be. I needed activity, distraction, anything to make the time pass quickly, so I called out to God, "I feel so alone and time hangs heavy on me with nothing to do," and in a flash He spoke to my spirit and said, "Why don't you write poetry." Write poetry? I could not believe what I'd heard. Write poetry? "I can't," was my response, "I've never been able to." Still He impressed it on my mind so I thought I should remind Him of how I had struggled with it at school without success. I just could not compose a poem. God was asking what for me was an impossibility but as he insisted, I got up, got my notepad and pen from my bag, got back into bed propped up on pillows, turned to a blank page, raised the pen poised over the page and thought, and waited. Nothing. "Told you so," I said. I knew I could not do it and had proved my point. I thought that would be the end of that, but how wrong was I? Slowly, gently, insistently He said those words again, "write poetry". By this time I must admit to a feeling of irritation the result of an overwhelming anxiety and feelings of inadequacy at being asked to do what I felt incapable of doing. Then it occurred to me that this was no ordinary request. God knew of my difficulties in this area, so if He was asking me to write, He must intend to give me something to write about. Irritation rapidly turned to anticipation as I again held the pen poised above the blank page, "OK God, I'm waiting." Then *wham*. Three sentences popped into my mind and I repeated them a few times. They were very profound. I pondered them for a while and thought, wow. I frantically wrote them down, afraid I might forget them, and then said, "OK Lord, what next?" and in a flash another sentence joined those on the pad. Words now flooded my mind and I struggled to capture them all on paper. Finally, I came to an end and read it through, it was very good. I had read it through several times before I realised it was good because it was a reflection of my emotions. The confusion and turmoil within had found expression in written verse. I could not have said it better if I had tried.

Foolishly now I thought I would give God a further test, and turned to a new page and held the pen in readiness. Words came, flowed, another page and another poem. I could not believe what had just happened. I looked about the ward and wondered if the other patients realised that they were in the midst of a miracle. It felt unreal but the evidence before my eyes was proof enough. I sat back and pondered what I had written with God's help. It was all about feelings, my emotions, about events that were unfolding in my life that caused me to feel extremely vulnerable on several planes.

After a while I lay there and wondered at this amazing, all-powerful God that I served and slowly dozed off. I reached for the pad and pen as I woke up and again turned to a new page and thought "let's see if I can still do it" and words flowed as my pen glided rapidly across the page. I wanted to know just how long God would continue in this way because although I was writing about my feelings, it was really God who was the mastermind behind it all. It was a foolish thought because of course God can keep it up indefinitely if He chose to. I scrolled back to the beginning and numbered the poems; each one that I wrote brought with it a measure of healing and by the end of the 3-day admission I had written nineteen poems. I smile now as I remember that the first thing I did each morning on the ward was to arm myself with pad and pen and wait for inspiration, and like clockwork, words filled my mind. I have continued to write poetry since. Some have been inspired by nature, others by a powerful word during morning worship etc. I have also been inspired to write for special occasions, weddings, and at various times, God revealed his truths in verse...these I have shared with the church.

Poetry was only the beginning for me. Almost a year to the day since I first began to write, my life changed drastically, late one evening when my husband, returning from a business trip told me our marriage of nineteen years was over. As you would expect, I was devastated. Two weeks later, he was gone. Our children then thirteen and sixteen were in shock. Getting through each day was like climbing a mountain without equipment, knowledge of its geography or training. But my ever-faithful Father told me what to do at every painful step. I sang and praised my way through a sea of turmoil and found relief. Several months later, as I drove home from work, I was struck by the faithfulness and loving kindness of God. I looked back to where I had been and where He had brought me to, and knew that although I had a long way to go, I would make it.

I had His promise and this overwhelming sense of joy that God loved me and was standing by me. I wanted to shout, sing, praise, thank him but could find no words that quite expressed what I felt so I cried in frustration, "God give me a song to sing your praise," and in seconds, I was singing at the top of my voice. I sang the same few sentences over and over again until I came to traffic lights and had to stop the car. Still singing, I rummaged for pen and paper, found a receipt, and began to write the words down. The lights changed and I moved on, but slowed at sight of every set of lights hoping they would change to red so I could write more. As I repeated the words, others were added.

When I got to Tesco car park, I needed to buy groceries, I wrote it all down but it was not complete, I knew there was more to come. In the supermarket I sang softly and hummed the verse and chorus I had with a wide smile on my face although I did not realise I was smiling until I noticed several people were smiling at me and greeting me. I smiled back of course, said "hello" and wondered where we had met. After a while I became aware that I was smiling broadly and had a spring to my steps. After some effort to control my voice and face, I gave up, shopped quickly and rushed for the car where I promptly bust forth in loud uncontrolled singing all the way home. I hummed my verse and chorus to God all evening and when I finally retired to bed, sat propped up on pillows with pen and pad and said, "OK Lord, I need the rest," and He gave it to me. I sang it to my local fellowship the following Sunday morning as my testimony to God.

I did not pursue song writing but on another occasion, four years later, while listening to Gospel Tonight on cable TV, there was such a volley of wonderfully inspired songs that as I worshipped, I again was at a loss for words and said, "Lord I should write a song. What can I write?" I focused on what I wanted to say but nothing came. I tried various beginnings but got no further and then the Holy Spirit impressed on me that it needed to come out of my experience. So I cast my mind back over my life and the words came and flowed. I wrote two songs that night. I have done nothing with them yet. I feel they must be sung but I must wait on God for the time, venue and medium through which they will be shared with the body of Christ.

Between both those experiences, I had another that was the beginnings of an answer to a childhood dream. I worked as a community support worker for adults with learning disabilities, and on this occasion, had accompanied a client to the theatre to see Saturday Night Fever. From what I saw of it, it was a great show, because right in the middle of a fabulous song and dance routine, I heard a barrage of words buzzing around in my ear. They painted a vivid picture and I visualised a scene of a young woman overcoming great odds to succeed, a bit like my own recent history to some extent. I knew immediately that I had the beginnings of the novel I had always wanted to write and I had to record it, but the only paper I had was the program I had bought. I found a pen in my handbag, and in semi-darkness, began to write squinting and using the index finger of my left hand as a guide for each new line. I hoped it would be legible on top of the printed sheet and also that I had not written one line on top of another. I could not wait for the intermission when I could check what I had done.

At last they broke for refreshments, I assisted my client to make a few purchases, got her settled comfortably, and was free to read through what I had written. I said, "Lord, this is great." I read it through again all the while I was thinking, I've begun my novel, finally I've begun my novel. I marvelled at the complexities of life and how in the midst of it all, God intervenes, does the most amazing things and makes them seem commonplace. I mean, who would be excited to write over a program they had bought, in semi-darkness, unconcerned that they had missed a whole chunk of the show? Everything seemed to take on another perspective, musical performances come and go, but the fulfilment of a lifetime dream will wait for no one.

When I was finally through with writing, I realised I had begun at the end. I had written the beginnings of the epilogue. Inspiration to build on it was few and far between, though it was never far from my mind. Several years passed with no progress. Then one day in 2004 I decided to take a week off work and visit a friend in Portsmouth. My daughter said I should take a notebook with me and continue with the novel. Unknown to her that had been my plan, and I'd told God about it and asked Him to inspire me to complete the epilogue and work my way back to the beginning. I had no clear idea how to write, or what to write, I just depended on God.

On my first full day in Portsmouth I had written for 4 1/2 hrs. By the end of my five-day break I had completed the epilogue, worked my way back to the beginning. My main character was the middle of five children of parents who held traditional values, and was a teenager looking in all the wrong places for love. Progress is slow but I continue to add to it.

God had heard the prayer of a 12-13 year old girl, understood the longing of her heart and orchestrated her life with precision to enable her to fulfil her dreams. Yes, the writing is on the wall in more ways than one. And if you're reading this book, then it has moved from the wall to the bookshelf. Praise the name of the Lord!

Choices, Choices

··•●•··

I mentioned above that I was at the lowest point in my life. That was in March 1998. It had been a difficult year for us, but at the end, following a mini cruise to celebrate our nineteenth wedding anniversary, I felt we had come through a very rough patch and could now continue to work toward a hopefully long and happy future. Separation and divorce were not the options I had ever dreamed would be placed before me. We were both Christians and as such, I fully believed that God could turn any situation around. I believed in the vows I took before God and man and had worked hard to fulfil them. I soon realised however, that my husband no longer believed or held the same values we had started our marriage with. His years of learning had opened his mind to other options he implied. I was therefore devastated when in March 1999 he said he no longer loved me, did not want to continue our marriage and was leaving, providing me with grounds for divorce.

I said I was devastated and that is one hundred percent true, however when I tell you that his news was not unexpected, you might wonder how this could be. Well, because we had not long come through a rough patch, when I was informed of the work opportunity that would take him from home for a whole month. I questioned the wisdom of accepting the offer. My concerns were pushed aside and he left for Jamaica on 3rd February 1999.

While he was gone, I set myself the task of redecorating the living/dining room with one of my younger sisters' help. She taught me how to cut and hang wallpaper, matching the pattern, and to put up a border. Between us we did a great job. Prior to our decorating binge, in the second week of my husband's absence, I was in the kitchen one day when I heard, *your husband is coming home and he will say that he's leaving*. It was as though someone was standing just behind me to the right and had spoken in my ear and as though swatting a fly, I brushed the words away while at the same time looking over my shoulder and wondering where such a thought had come from. In the third week of his trip in an almost identical situation, I again heard those words and my response was the same only this time I thought I was frightening myself by dwelling on the past year instead of trusting God for the future. But when four or five days before he returned I was once more in the kitchen when God spoke clearly and insistently and His voice filled my head and sank into the very depth of my heart...*your husband is coming home, he will tell you he has had time to think, and that he is leaving.* I cried, "Oh God, what is this you are telling me? If this is so, please give me the strength to bear it." And He did, because those words were burnt on my mind and in my thoughts day and night until he returned; but on every occasion when I thought of them, I had this sense of over-whelming peace. It was after this that my sister came up for a day and we actually began to decorate the rooms. We talked and laughed, listened to music and ate – all very normal things. As I did so, I wondered how I could be behaving so naturally when my world was about to explode? But that deep-rooted peace did not leave me.

On 5th March 1999 at 10.35p.m. the doorbell rang and I knew it was my husband. I was putting the boarders up, had sticky hands and wondered why he did not use his key. I opened up for him and felt surprise that I did not greet him affectionately as I had done for nineteen years but just stepped back to allow him in, turned and walked away back into the living room. He had dropped his suitcase and briefcase in the hall and followed me into the living room. He looked stressed, upset, began to remove his coat and launched into his speech, "you won't like what I am going to say but I have to say it. I have had time to think. I don't love you and I am leaving." This all took place within a minute of his entering the house. I looked at him and felt pity at his distress. He sat on the sofa and I placed an arm about his shoulder patting and trying to comfort him. It was strange because all the while I was doing so I was also having an internal conversation with myself asking, "What are you doing? Remove your hand from his shoulder, why should he be comforted when your heart is breaking?" But I could not stop. I remembered that God had prepared me, had strengthened me, that I loved this man that was so upset and fearful of the future. I was puzzled too that his revelation brought him so much distress, yet when I offered a logical solution, taking it to God and allowing Him to deal with it, it was rejected.

Without going into detail, he later revealed his spiritual condition which was shocking to me because I had not seen it, although several things had puzzled me and I had prayed and asked God for wisdom in them. How a man or woman moves away from God is not important except to mankind. That he/she has moved away is enough. God calls all disobedience sin but we tend to measure or put different values on it. That he had fallen, there was no doubt. Who was I to judge? It was upsetting, it was even shocking but the greatest shock to me was his refusal to repent, seek God's forgiveness and turn away from sin. When I realised this, it was the end of my attempts to comfort him. Briefly then, he refused the wise counsel of our mothers, my Pastor, our Christian friends and myself. His mind was made up and two weeks later he was gone.

Needless to say, it was a very difficult time for all, especially our children. I was angry for them. My emotions were all over the place and my constant prayer was, "Father, please make me strong for them," and each time I prayed I received a new outpouring of the Spirit to strengthen me.

There is one occasion that stands out in my mind during the period immediately following his revelation that greatly encouraged and strengthened me. I was told my marriage was over on Wednesday 5th March, on Monday 10th March we had an unexpected guest and his surname was 'Victory'. Now some might say I made too much of it but only I knew what I was going through and the ceaseless conversations I was having with God to get through each day.

This Pastor from New York had made a trip to England for the first time, accepting the invitation of a Christian friend he had met in New York. I think he came hoping to see a bit of the country and to take up preaching engagements for ten days. However, when he arrived at Heathrow Airport, he realised he had lost the contact number of the person he was to stay with who was to arrange an itinerary for him. He knew no one else in England. He rang home, was given the number of my husband's grandfather in New York who then gave him our number and he called. He had called several times and left messages on the answer machine. We had actually gone to my mother where my husband informed her of the situation and of his decision to leave. This gentleman had arrived at the airport in the morning, had tried all day to contact us, could not get a flight back to New York until the following day, and had decided to call us one last time before arranging an overnight stay at a hotel before returning home. We had just arrived home at 7.00p.m. and I had just placed the key in the door when the phone began to ring. I rushed in and answered it. A voice said, "my name is...Victory," and more besides, but I hardly heard it. The visit to my mother had been hard on me, I was feeling sore and wondering how I would cope and asking God to "please help," and the next thing I knew a man called 'Victory' was speaking to me. I felt an inner leaping and heard myself say, "God has brought victory to my home." I didn't know if he had heard me and I remember thinking that if he had he must have thought that I was nuts. He explained his difficulty and without thinking or consulting my husband, I invited him to stay with us. I told him how to use public transport to get to our local train station where I would meet him, informing him of what I would be wearing so he could identify me. I then told my husband what had happened and of my response. He was annoyed at my invitation "with things as they are," he said, but I had not really considered it. How could I not extend hospitality to one in need and God's servant? I was also convinced that God had sent him to us for this time but what I said was, "that we could not do otherwise".

Almost immediately our guest knew something was wrong and said as much. I confided in him and thereafter he took on the role of counsellor and friend to the children and me. My husband went out early and came in late to avoid any conversation with him. He was an excellent counsellor and helped us to talk about what was happening and how we felt. Until then, apart from my initial conversation with them and the reassurances I'd given, I had tip toed around the subject. I did not speak to them about it as I did not know what to say so had concentrated on going on as usual and keeping things as normal as possible in what was to us all a very abnormal situation. Every so often I would find myself staring at our guest. I don't think he was aware of it as I tried to be discrete. What no-one knew was that every time I looked at him, I heard God's promise to "try me and prove me, with me you are safe," and at that moment in time this Pastor from New York was an unwitting tool in God's hand in the fulfilment of His promise.

Some might ask, "How did God keep you safe if your marriage is ended?" Well, fortunately, because He is God, he gave us freedom to choose and we don't always make the right decisions or stand by the ones we make, but God always stands by his! He (God) asked me a question one evening after my husband had left and I was feeling quite distressed and praying he would return home. He first revealed to me the full state of his unrepentant heart, the fact that whatever the outward appearance, he had turned completely away from God. He said "if you could have him back in his present state as I have revealed it to you would you choose to have him," and he opened my mind to the kind of life I and our children would have to compromise with...*or would you remain with me?* And I knew it was not an option for me. I imagined life with my husband, the man God revealed, and I considered life without him as I was experiencing it. I then considered life with God as I knew it, and I tried to imagine life without Him. I could not. It would not be worth having! I understood clearly that what God had shown me was that my husband posed a real danger to my walk with him and the salvation of our children that I was praying for. It was difficult to accept this but God revealed that unless he repented and turned back to God, he would always serve other gods.

The bible says if your right arm offends you, cut it off. Whatever will keep us from the kingdom we should be willing to give it up. I therefore resigned myself to the reality of being the head of a single parent household. God was my father and my prayer and hope was that he would one day be my children's Father too. He will always be first in my life, my first love.

Healing

Weeks after my husband had left, back at work (I had taken two weeks off) and going through the motions of normalcy, I found myself fighting a battle of the mind and I was losing ground. I was angry, bitter, crying out for and really desiring revenge for the hurt he had inflicted on us, for the rejection we were all struggling with. I did not recognise myself. Outwardly nothing seemed to have changed but inside where God could see, I was a mess! I fought hard but it seemed that at every turn some new revelation had undermined the relationship and marriage I had thought I had.

The betrayal was devastating. I had been made to live a lie for how long only God knew. I seemed to be asking for forgiveness for my thoughts all day long. It was wearying. I could even have conversations about very spiritual things while my mind was sinking into a morass of spiritual suicide. I recognised my danger immediately and had put up a good fight but needed help. I was receiving counsel from my pastor regularly and told him of this new front I was struggling with. I also requested

172

prayer at our Friday night prayer meetings and also of close friends. I began to win more than I lost and was reminded by the Holy Spirit of the power of praise. I would wake with praise and thanksgiving on my lips. I sang praise with the help of a few choice cassettes all the way to work and back and for those periods during the day when I was in my car on my way to see a client.

At the first recognition of a thought pattern that did not glorify the Father I would burst into song. At the first feeling of heaviness I began to praise. At the first negative thought at what I had lost I began to thank for what I had. It was not easy. I did not feel like doing any of those things initially. But I soon noticed that the battles were fewer and shorter, the victory sweeter and more enduring. It got to a point when people would want to know how I managed to remain so strong and my response was always the same. God was my strength!

God was very gentle with me during this time. There was much to learn, much to change, much to do but I could only manage one thing at a time. The first thing that He brought to my attention was the fact that I had placed a barrier between Him and myself. I was feeling particularly vulnerable at this time, had many unanswered questions and had gone before God in prayer. I had not got far when He said, "how can I hear you when you have placed a barrier between us?" And as He spoke, I became aware that all my words had remained in the room as though suspended below the ceiling. "What barrier Lord?" I asked, "What have I done?" He revealed that I held anger toward my husband, that I had allowed bitterness to take root. He told me that for as long as I would not forgive, He could not forgive or hear me when I prayed. "But Lord," I said "he has not even repented. He has not said he was sorry or asked for me to forgive him." And God replied, "what if he never does, will you put your salvation in jeopardy waiting on him? Your anger, bitterness and un-forgiveness will not hurt him but it will destroy you." God revealed how Satan would use this tactic against me, and ultimately our children because if I backslid too, who would be their example? Who would teach them the truth? He reminded me that Satan aims his attack strategically, at the leader of the church, the shepherd, so the flock would scatter, at the head of the family so the home would be divided etc. Satan wanted me dead, ineffective, my family lost.

I saw his subtlety and my danger and ran to the cross. I recognised that forgiveness was not based on feelings, on whether or not I felt like forgiving, or it being requested of me, but on choice, on knowing what was right and doing it, as God requires of us all. Right there on my knees I confessed my sin and chose to forgive. Then God said, I know, and you know, that you have forgiven him, but he should know too." I wrote my husband a letter to that effect and also told him when he phoned one day. I got no response to either. I did not expect it, and it did not matter. I had obeyed my Father and the barrier was removed.

I began to do better, to feel better, whole. God began to show me that I placed too much value on what my husband, or anyone else for that matter, thought or said of me. It was what my Father thought of and said of me that should take pre-eminence. And what did He say, that I was His heir, that He loved me, would not leave or forsake me, would keep me safe, had a place prepared for me, and so much more. He caused me to re-evaluate my life and that which he had called me to be. He made me see that although I was not perfect and had made mistakes, my intentions had been good, the wellbeing of my family foremost. He told me that I had to be strong, that I was now the head of the home with all the responsibility that that entailed, and that I was to continue to live the life of a believer before our children. I was to continue to set them a good example and teach them the ways of God that they might know that it was possible to stay the course. God said it was important that they knew that He was faithful, that He kept His word, that He would provide for our needs, that He could be trusted. He said that they would learn these things by observing my life. I was on the road to healing. My purpose was clear. Our children and the world would know by my life that God was faithful.

God made his faithfulness very clear to me one day when in prayer and supplication I had expressed the feeling of shock and disbelief at my changed circumstances. I had cried out to the Lord that I felt as if the rug had been pulled out from under me and I was free falling; even on my knees I felt unsteady. But do you know what God, by His Spirit, said? *The rug may have been pulled from under your feet, but I am under the rug, so stand.* It was a command and no sooner said than I felt solid ground under my feet and I knew He would not let me fall. I would stand because He was standing with me. I would stand because He was holding me up. I would stand because I could see and feel His hand under me.

I went before God in supplication for the salvation of our children. I knew about generation curses and was concerned on their behalf. God led me to a passage, a whole chapter on the issue and when I had read it, I was comforted. Not long after, one Sunday evening, we visited Bethel Ministries in Hammersmith, where one of my older brothers is the Elder. There he prophesied over our daughter and told me not to be concerned for our son. I will not go into the prophecy or word at this point except to say that their lifestyles as they grew would have discouraged me if I had not known that not one word of The One who gives promises ever falls to the ground empty.

The Everlasting Arms

··•●•··

I had many conversations with my Father as you can imagine and He was always right there any time, day or night. He had led me to pray and fast for seven consecutive days for my family. I had prayed and fasted for my husband and children. My husband who was unrepentant, my daughter, who was angry and refused to pray or attend church, and for my son who was silent, said he was OK, but clearly was not. Through it all God had surrounded me with his love and kept His promises uppermost in my mind.

Although I had resigned myself to singleness, for a time at least, because I had not fully given up on my marriage and still hoped my husband would recognise his error and seek after God, I continued to pray for him, I knew God was ready to receive him. Then came the day and a realisation and acceptance that it would not happen and I began to feel very lonely even with my children around me, in the midst of my extended family and in the midst of a crowd. I felt the need to be hugged and told I was loved. I could not tell anyone how I felt so

I told God one Sunday morning on my knees, in my bedroom and He responded miraculously later that morning at church.

Most of the older members of my local church, older in years of membership not age, knew that I preferred a handshake to a hug although I never refused to hug or be hugged when appropriate. Generally, most people greeted each other with an embrace. I extended my hand and they accepted it in love. On this particular Sunday morning I had expressed my longing to God in prayer privately at home. That morning in church I had gone forward for prayer for my husband and children and two ladies approached me to pray. At the end of their prayers of agreement one of the ladies said, "I know you don't like to be hugged but I'm going to give you one anyway." And she embraced me in a tight embrace and I of course did the same. But there was no end to her embrace so I made a movement that ordinarily indicated that it was time to part. She paid no attention to my cue so I continued to hang on thinking that maybe she was in need of an embrace herself so held her more closely! After a little while I again attempted to bring it to an end but she would have none of it! I was surprised and puzzled. This was not very British behaviour and totally uncharacteristic of this person.

As I considered these things and pondered what was happening, like a light turned on I realised I had moved on from feeling her slim arms around me to feeling that I was engulfed in massive arms that did not appear to have an end. I felt it warm from my earlobes right down to my ankles, warm and soft and comforting, and I felt so safe and secure. As I marvelled at what was happening, I could see something being poured out of a glass jug, a clear liquid that glowed and I felt it entering me. It was love, so much love was being poured into my soul that I felt full to overflowing. When I grasped what God was doing in response to my prayer, I just broke down and sobbed. I cried, and cried, and cried some more, because my Father was hugging me and telling me how much He loved me. It was wonderful. When eventually I realised I had soaked Sue's blouse I started fumbling for a tissue and was given one. Pretty soon it was soaked through but I could not stop. Her shoulder was completely soaked and still she would not let me go and I knew she could not. My head seemed to lie on a massive shoulder that did not tire and I just rested and gave over all the repressed emotions and longings of my heart to Him. When my tears eventually dried, I felt as light as a feather yet filled with love. I tried to apologise for the wet blouse but all she said was 'it's alright' and still held me but now I realised why her behaviour was so out of character. God had chosen to use her in a special way to convey to me his love. It was His arms I'd felt, it was His shoulder I'd cried on and it was His love that was poured into me!

The other lady, who had also prayed for me was silent through all this but when the embrace finally ended and we took a step back from each other she spoke to me. This is what she said, "God wants you to know that *it was not in vain.*" This was truly amazing because that very morning I had been asking him if all the years of loving, giving, sacrificing for my husband and family had been in vain; if all the nurturing, role modelling and praying for our children's salvation had been in vain. I could see no positive signs anywhere but that morning He made me to know that *it was not in vain.* And so, I became strong. I held on to every one of His words and promises over my life and that of my children. I verbalised them in prayer and rejoiced at what would be and learned to be expectant but patient. I have never felt lonely since and as far as human companionship and love goes, I have not felt a need for it. Even so, as I was only in my mid-forties then, I did not think I'd want to be alone always so I gave this thought into my Father's hands. His will for my life is what I seek, whatever that entails, it is what I accept gladly. He has placed me in green pastures. I no longer yearn after what I do not or cannot have. I rejoice in what I have and what is before me according to His promises over my life and that of my children.

In my distress had God kept his promise? YES! In more ways than I can number and now many years on, I can truly say that I have never felt that longing, that need for human contact, that need to be loved as I did back then. God's love filled me; He gave me something that day that was permanent and beyond expression.

From party girl to Helper

·· • ··

Our daughter's attachment to her father began in the womb. He was sure I would have a
little girl and he had been right. Her name
was my choice. I was a great fan of the Roma-
nian gymnast of the 1976 Olympics who repeatedly scored the perfect 10. I had also seen
a South African Musical Production 'Ipi Tombi'
at the theatre three times. One of the actors
had sung a beautiful song to his wife who had
the same name, and that had sealed it for me.
If and when I had a daughter, that would be
her name. However, I chose to change its
spelling to give it a unique touch as my daughter would be unique. Her relationship with her
father seemed to confirm research that had
indicated that you could communicate with the
unborn baby and that they recognised voices.
She certainly knew her father's and responded
to it immediately. I had accepted their close-
ness but frequently prayed for a closer relationship with her myself. It was not that we
did not have a good relationship, just that
when her father was present they were inseparable.

As she grew and her father became more and more caught up in his work, career, various committees etc. I knew that she felt rejected by him, as he seemed to have little or no time for her, or her brother. This was in stark contrast to what she had been used to and she was naturally upset. She could not understand why he did not have time for her and she retreated away from everyone. I made every effort to draw his attention to the situation and prayed about it constantly. Very little progress was made and I was at a loss to understand his behaviour. While he said all his efforts were for us, I would point out that it was his presence and attention that we needed, the children especially, and his daughter particularly because of their close bond. By the time our son had arrived on the scene, he was already very busy so that he had developed a closer bond with me and chose my company over his father's generally. The complete opposite to his sister! I never gave up trying to draw close to her to make up, in part, for her father's lack of attention, but she would generally push me away, not so much by her words, but more by her attitude, even when very young. I suppose her reasoning was that if she couldn't have her dad, she wouldn't have me either, or her brother for that matter! They did not get on, mostly because she kept him at arm length despite his wanting to be friends with her. I saw her frequent hurt but could do nothing to ease it but pray and ask God for an answer while continuing my efforts with my husband. She was a lonely child in many ways and this hurt me, as I did not seem to be able to help her.

You can imagine then, with this history, how she felt when her father told her he was leaving the marriage, and by extension leaving her, and, ten days later, left. She told me later that it was like being rejected a second time. And she rejected God. She was sixteen years old and had been full of questions. Deep down she knew God to be real and unconsciously reached out to him every time she opened her mouth and sang praise and worship songs straight from the heart in her bedroom. She had done this regularly from an early age. Now she did not care and would go her own way. She refused to attend counselling to discuss how she felt about his leaving and she would not talk about it with me either. She hid it in some deep dark place in her heart and put a lid firmly on it. She didn't even cry! She was dealing with her hurt as she had always done, by burying it.

As usual I turned to God for the answer and he provided it, although at first it seemed the exact opposite to what I had asked for. She stopped attending church and she refused to participate in family prayers. Her brother at thirteen would have done the same if he could. He was there in body only because, at his age, I could insist. Eventually I was on my own. They were not interested in talking to or hearing from God. They thought, if he was not powerful enough to keep their dad from leaving, if he could not prevent him from turning away, "What was the point?"

Our daughter started going to nightclubs with her unsaved friends. She bought clothing for these events and dressed her hair to suit. She began to experiment with make up to finish off the look (thank goodness it bore no resemblance to war paint but was tastefully done). I looked at my beautiful child and cringed inwardly. We had the occasional battle of wills where I would insist on an item of clothing being returned to the shop because it could not possibly perform the function of covering anything! I was informed that I was old fashioned and needed to get with the times. I was informed that this was normal dress sense and that everyone dressed like that, etc. etc. I was thankful that I at least had details of where she was going and who with, but she rarely returned at the stated times. She pushed boundaries. I reinforced them. She knew and I think resented the fact that I hedged her about with prayer. I ensured I called her by name when I prayed so she'd know I would not give up on her, she'd know I was interested in her well-being and that while I may not be able to control her behaviour, I would not accept it or change because she wanted me to. I made sure that she was aware of the possible dangers out there and advised her on how to avoid them, how to manage situations. I also assured her that she could call on/come to me at any time no matter the situation, I would be there if she needed me. What more could I do? I'd never been to a nightclub myself but knew enough of what went on to not want any child of mine participating. When she went out, I would go to bed but did not sleep until I knew she was home again. This was a difficult time for me but I was not alone. God gave me strength and His words over her life served to focus my prayers.

As stated, because I could not prevent her from going to these places, I hedged her about with prayers and did so after every click of the closing door. My prayer took this form, "Lord, as she goes let your covering extend from her neck to wrist to ankle, let her appear plain, let those with wrong intentions who would seek to do harm not see her, do not let shame be her portion, she is your child...let no danger attach itself to her, and bring her safely home, in Jesus name. Amen." I also prayed that she would remember all my warnings regarding drinks and drugs, about making her own purchase, not leaving it unattended, not returning to it, not trying anyone else's drink etc. I bored her with these rules and much more every time she went out. I was not going to make it easy for her to enjoy herself so another of my prayer was: "Lord, please do not allow her to enjoy herself at this club/rave so that she loses her desire to attend them and turn to you, I pray in Jesus Name, Amen."

When boyfriends were added to the equation, I insisted on meeting them (to make it clear to them the home she was coming from and my expectations). My strategy remained the same; I got on my knees and spoke my heart to my Father. "Lord, this young man is not saved; cause her to end this relationship. Let the breaking come from her so she does not feel another man has rejected her and compound her hurt. In Jesus Name, amen.". Although she had not accepted Christ as her Lord and Saviour, I know her heart was seeking him desperately even while she appeared to be rejecting Him. I knew salvation was just around the corner. Three times I prayed that prayer and God heard and answered. She ended three relationships, nice young men each one, but not Christians therefore, not for my daughter. You may wonder why I prayed as I did. The answer is simple. My daughter had craved and lacked the attention of her father and was, subconsciously, attempting to replace him under the guise that it was normal at her age to have a boyfriend. Culturally it was not normal for me and I had not raised her to expect any different. Spiritually it was not natural and I had raised her in the knowledge of God and His commands and expected her to abide by them, even though she had not made a commitment to God yet. Additionally, I felt that until she had dealt with the emotional turmoil in her heart, built up over the years, she was not fit to enter any relationship. She carried too much baggage. Of course, she was also too young and lacked maturity for any such relationship and these young men, naturally, were not Christians and would have a world view of what a relationship was and entailed. Basically then, I was out to keep her, by God's grace, safe, to keep her from making a terrible and irreversible mistake and adding to her troubles.

God had given a prophetic word over her life when she was sixteen following much prayer and fasting on my part after her father had left. He had made it clear that she would try to walk the path her friends walked, but it was not the path for her. He would draw her on to the path he had for her. She heard these prophetic words and dismissed them rebelliously, but I'd held them close to me and confessed them in prayer each time I raised her up before the Lord and each time she acted contrary to His word.

So, there she was dressed up to the nines and going off to raves fairly regularly, though no more than once a fortnight at my insistence. She was still a student and I kept her focussed on her education and goals. And there I was on my knees, covering her with prayer. I made it a practice to ask her how the rave went each time, whether she had enjoyed herself, had fun. At first the answers were "yes", "great" and so on; but it was not long before they were less enthusiastic. Then I noticed that she went less often and sometimes made excuses to her friends not to attend. I made no comment outwardly but I was bubbling with excitement inside. God was at work. Eventually her responses became, "it was ok", "I don't know why I went really", "I only went because I didn't want to disappoint my friends", "I wish I hadn't gone; it was a waste of time." By this time, I was spiritually leaping for joy, but very calm and sympathetic on the outside. She stopped going altogether. This happened over a period of about two years. Then came her battles with boredom, which had the power to reduce her to tears. Boredom is one of the worst things she could ever suffer, since she was a toddler.

I began to notice that sometimes, when I returned from church, she would ask questions about the meeting in such a way as to deny any real interest. Then too, on rare occasions she would say casually, "I might come to church with you tomorrow," or "save a seat for me, I'll meet you there," and I, just as casually, would say "OK", hiding my excitement. This new development was the beginning of sleepless nights for me. She had so many questions and none of them required answering before midnight, except on rare occasions. I would be having some great dream (always full of adventure) when I would become aware that I was not alone in my bedroom, and opening my eyes, would see her either standing by or sitting on my bed. My soul would cry, "No, not now," while my heart ached to help her find what she was looking for.

She is a deep thinker and everything had to make sense; one plus one always equalled two. But, when she applied this formula to spiritual matters, it just did not compute; and so, my troubles began and I would wave goodbye to sleep. She so wanted to understand God so that she could trust him! At the end of one of these one, two, three-hour sessions I would feel completely drained and did not even have the satisfaction of knowing that I had resolved her problem. Where I successfully answered one question, two or three more would raise their heads. It took me right back to her childhood when she naturally had lots and lots of questions to which she would generally responded to my answers with why? No matter how much information I gave her, she would still ask why? These sessions always ended with her saying, "thanks mum" and going off to bed where she'd immediately settle into some form of comatose sleep all her troubles temporarily relieved, while I would lie wide awake all hope of sleep long gone.

When she was about eight or nine years old with a million questions already under her belt and my brain fried to a frazzle, I had a brainwave, what little there was left. I decided that the very next time she asked a question, I would no longer tailor the answer to her immediate need, but would expand it into a mixture of past, present and future. Taking her back into the history or origins of the subject at hand, tie it in to the present and project into the future as the case may be. Suffice to say she got more than she bargained for. Every possible question that might have risen to her lips (I saw them clearly) was answered without her even voicing them. The first time I did this I struggled to keep the laughter out of my voice at the look of horror on her face when I just went on and on about things she had not even asked. She was struck dumb, literally, for a while because at the end she just turned and walked away. It was days before she asked another question and the funniest thing was, that when she realised what she had done, she looked horrified and distressed at the same time and shifted her weight on her legs un-comfortably to wait for my very long answer. Tears of laughter stinging the back of my eyes, I turned away so she would not see my quivering lips, and taking pity on her, gave a brief, concise answer. Her relief was patent!

So, I suffered in silence for little over a year, always in the knowledge of where her search would end. I would sometimes ask, "Lord, why now, at one o'clock in the morning when we'd been chatting about all sorts of unimportant things earlier that evening?"

She finally committed her life to Jesus and was baptised aged 20 years old to my great joy and relief! We still had long chats in my bedroom late at night but the times were more reasonable. She sings even more now and there is an anointing on her voice, which moves you at the hearing. She was very active at her church and keen to serve. She has recently gone full circle and returned to the fellowship she attended as a child. She still has questions because God saw fit to give her an enquiring mind. Thank God not all her questions are directed at me, she has an outlet via bible study. We are now very close and great friends. This change in our relationship began to take shape in her late teens following the prophetic word I mentioned earlier. Also instrumental I think was the way I responded to the news that one of her friends was pregnant, it seems it was in great contrast to the girls' parents (also Christians) who were unforgiving, ready to disown their daughter, made her life a misery and threatened to put her out. Via my daughter I offered shelter to this young woman should she need it and advised my daughter on how best she could support her friend. This had a massive impact on her and she began to draw closer to me. She later told me that my response helped her to know how to recognise a true Christian. She began to seek my advice and took it even when it was difficult. What we have today is all I had asked God for and more. She had informed me that I was not an easy mum to have that I was hard and unyielding, that she hated the boundaries I set around her, that she resented it when I would not let her do the things her friends were allowed, that her friends and their mums were friends. I listened to it all and informed her that God had not asked me to be her friend but her mother; that the relationships and responsibilities between friends and parents were very different, and that I believed it was important to be a parent to my child first and foremost, and a friend second. We are great friends today with the respect due me as a mother firmly in place. She is an inspiration and source of encouragement to me and provides timely reminders when I am slacking in any area where she knows God has required me to act. She is my unofficial, unpaid personal assistant, my little big helper. "My right hand."

He is a man now Lord, I give him back!

···•●•···

You will remember that when our son was ill with meningitis, and after much prayer with no obvious result, God had reminded me that while he was my son, God had gifted him to me because he was God's son before he was ever mine...very true. Well time had passed and things had changed. I was now separated from his father who had left home a week after his thirteenth birthday and was now actively seeking a divorce. It had been a difficult time for us. Outwardly, there was little to notice in our son's behaviour but he was fighting a silent war and the first I knew of it was when he barricaded himself in his room and trashed it. There are still dents in the plaster of his bedroom wall where he'd try to put his fist through it. He was angry with God who had revealed the breakup of the marriage to him in dreams over a year before and he had been praying continually for God to intervene. He did not answer in the way he'd expected so he rejected God and blamed himself for not being able to save the marriage and protect me. When he confided in me, I was shocked at the burden he had been carrying for so long at such a young age; and touched that he had been trying to protect me from hurt because "he knew I loved dad". Unlike his sister, he agreed to receive counselling. I arranged for him to see a Christian counsellor and he had one session only then refused to have any more. He knew he could continue any time he chose and I would support him through it but he did not choose to. A few years later I received a letter from his school informing me of uncharacteristic behaviour and his referral to the youth counselling service. He was then fifteen years old.

He seemed to lose interest in his studies. He had never been a keen student but had always done fairly well and left school at sixteen with good GCSE's. He enrolled at the local College to do his 'A' Levels, not because he particularly wanted to take them, but because I insisted. He had wanted to get a job, take a year out, and return to education later. I was concerned that once earning, he might not return to education at all, hence my insistence that he completed his 'A' levels before taking time out. He did not do well at college. Lacking motivation, he was not particularly interested in any of the subjects on offer at this level. Nothing I said or did made a difference. This went on for two years during which time he changed his subjects. I was frustrated and anxious for his future. We had several conversations about it but he felt I was nagging. What could I do? I had shared the difficulty I was experiencing with my extended family and pastor and they supported me in prayer and offered encouragement to him. I prayed about the situation so many times. I recalled in prayer God's promises for his life repeatedly. How could I let him alone, which is what he wanted, how was I to sit back and watch him make a mess of his life. I knew he was greatly discouraged by his father's absence and the contradictions that were apparent in what he had taught his son to be right and what he had chosen for himself at the expense of his family.

While he remained the well mannered, polite young man I had raised in many respects, the internal conflicts he experienced led to the development of habits that were regrettable, drinking, smoking (including the illegal stuff), stealing (sweets, just because he could and didn't care what happened to himself). To his credit, he recognised that he was headed in the wrong direction and tried to put an end to these things. Unsuccessful, he came to me for help. We prayed and fasted together often, he wanted to be accountable to me and he gave me permission to ask. His responses or lack of, frequently catapulted me into intense prayer. At times he would come to my room early in the morning or late at night (why do my children choose such anti-social times to unburden themselves) and just sit on the bed and say nothing. At times he'd flop sideways onto a pillow and just lie there. I'd say nothing, just wait and struggle into wakefulness if it were morning, or struggle to stay awake if it were night. Eventually I'd ask, "are you struggling?" He'd groan and I'd lay my hand on him and pray. On "amen" he'd be up and out and I'd say "just 5 more minutes Lord," if it were morning and bury myself under the duvet; or, "please help me to sleep Lord," if it were night, realising that I was now wide awake. And children are a gift

Thank God he was delivered from those habits.

One day, a few months after his eighteenth birthday I discussed his revision efforts or lack of with him and again was full of frustration because he was so casually unconcerned about his 'A' Levels. Walking into the kitchen trying to think of another approach and talking to

God I asked, "what more can I do?" He took me on a journey back to the hospital ward that our son had been admitted to, and to the toilet where I had prayed. He reminded me of my prayer, of my request that he took our child, his son, if he wanted him back, or give him back to me by making him well, if he wanted me to raise him to adulthood. It was as though a light bulb had been turned on. I knew exactly what I had to do and I did it! I said, "Lord, you heard my prayer that day and you gave him back to me. Here he is eighteen years old, an adult. I have done my bit as best I knew how; he is now a man and I can do no more so I give him back to you. He is yours to do what you will and fulfil your purpose for his life." I left it at that. He was now God's responsibility and I felt at ease with this, a peace settled on me and I was ready to watch developments with interest. What would God do? I don't know about you but I found this an exciting proposition. Two weeks later at a crusade that he attended to please me he gave his life to Jesus and his whole mindset and outlook changed. It was like seeing a child mature overnight; that was the level of change that was visible in him. Once again God had acted so swiftly that he took my breath away.

About one month later he told me that he would be leaving college at the end of the academic year without his 'A' levels and getting a job. I agreed because by now it was clear that I had been wrong to insist on his continuing his education. Two years had been wasted. Other more important issues, for him, had been going on and I had not taken time to talk them through with him, believing him to be too young to know what was right or good for him. He got a job with a mobile phone company. I was not surprised he went into sales. He had the knack for it and was enjoying his job. The change in him was great to see. Two weeks into this job and he came home bursting with excitement. He told me that he finally knew exactly what he wanted to do with his life and would be enrolling in college to study business the following year, and so he did!

But things did not always go smoothly for him and shortly before starting his course, a little over a year after his commitment to Christ, he turned away, making excuses for himself. God had already revealed to his Pastor and me that he would be coming under spiritual attack. The whole family were praying for him. My prayer was very short and to the point. I prayed, "Lord, don't let him be out there for months or years making a mess of his life. Let it be very short, weeks only. Let him realise his error and the devils' strategy to try to destroy him. Let him repent and come back to you."

I was in Portsmouth with an old school friend and her son, my godson, for a short break staying at a friends' flat in Port Solent, when I rang home early one Tuesday morning to speak to him before he left for work. He was pleased I had called. He had good news for me. He had repented and was forgiven. He apologised for his behaviour and thanked me for my prayers. He described how he had observed the hand of God drawing him back to where he knew he should be. God had heard and answered my prayer of faith immediately and it had only taken three weeks to become a physical reality. To God be given all the glory! God's hand on his life is clearly visible. He actively prays for and witnesses to his friends and has seen several of them come to the Lord. He has shared his testimony and the Word of God at youth meetings and seen young people, especially young men, saved. His zeal and maturity I watched with pleasure. It was a joy to see. I looked at him and he was the same and completely different all at once. Since he committed his life to Jesus, all my prayers concerning him have been answered and more, much more! As I said, his attitude and outlook were so different. His hard work at college had been commended and he has since graduated from university where he studied Business and Marketing. Under the guidance of his Pastor (also his uncle), he has engaged in training for ministry and is actively involved in youth ministry which is where is heart is.

This young man whose world fell apart when his father left and who, in his own words, "felt his security (wrapped up in his family) had vanished," had walked a hard and dangerous road. But for the grace of God, his life could have read like a horror story and counted as just another statistical measurement. Thank God who had a plan for him and is even now working it out. Isn't God amazing.

Revelation

·· ● ··

As mentioned before, my eldest brothers' fifti-
eth birthday bash was the occasion that
marked the full realisation of Gods' answer to
my prayer, salvation for my whole family.
Time went on and I continued to marvel at
Him, at His truth and faithfulness.

We are a close family. As children my parents,
mum especially, managed to bind us together
with the invisible glue of love. We share each
other's hopes, dreams, joys, sorrows and pain.
We support each other, help each other, and
pray for each other but oddly enough until
shortly before Christmas 2003 we had never
got together as Christians to pray except for a
few occasions.

Things were about to change. God encouraged
one of my sisters to call us to prayer. We all
met at her home and prayed for 2-3 hours, so-
cialised and then went our separate ways, but
before we did, she stated that, "this was the
beginning of many calls to prayer, it would be
a regular occurrence," or words to that effect.
We all agreed that it was the way forward but

strangely enough, we did not repeat the experience.

Then came March 2004 and a passing comment from my daughter in relation to one of my many nieces and difficulties being experienced. I suppose being a fairly gentle-hearted person I did not like to think of anyone in difficulty of any kind, especially one of my own. I thought about it and realised that to varying degrees, we were all going through different things and that we were living in difficult times. This realisation was quickly followed by a conviction that we needed to pray as, simultaneously, I heard a gentle but insistent voice say *you should all pray!* I knew that voice so I listened closely and to paraphrase, this is what He said, *you all have problems, and you are all under attack. Everyone is in their own corner praying but why should you pray alone. If one of you hurt, you all feel the pain. If one of you celebrates, you all rejoice. Shouldn't you do the same in trouble? If one of you prays, shouldn't you all pray? When each of you pray, I hear and answer, how much more could I do if you all prayed together...? What could I not do*! God was calling us to pray together as one, not 'individuals' for individual needs, but 'one' for all needs. I listened again and He continued, *I called you all to pray before and you started but did not continue.* He reminded me of my sister's words and revealed that we had all heard it, felt it was good and right, but had done nothing about it. We had left the onus on her to call us to prayer when in fact He (God) had already done so through her. He had said it should be a 'regular occurrence'. We had no excuse.

Again, He said that, we were *a blessed family, that He had invested in us many gifts of the Spirit which when brought together in Him in prayer would make of us a mighty army for the spiritual battle that was ahead. That, our children were under attack and we had the power and authority in Christ to go on the offensive, rather than the defensive from where we often fought. They were targets because Satan wanted to break the line of blessings they would inherit. He saw what God had in store for them and would stop at nothing to hinder them. The battle was at our door.*

I knew God was in earnest as only He could be and shared this revelation of His will for our family with my daughter Nadya. The next person I spoke to was my mother a few days later. When I shared with her what God had said to me, her response was immediate. She offered her home as the venue where we would all meet to pray. She then urged me to contact the rest of the family and set a date and time for the first meeting stressing that it should not be delayed. We had the first meeting three weeks later. Present were my mum, four brothers, three sisters, one sister in-law, one nephew and his wife and their son, my great nephew, and my daughter. Four generations, in one place, with one purpose.

Prior to the gathering I had sought God for instructions on how to move forward into this new area He was calling us to. I believe He wanted us to not only pray for each other and our families, but to pray for the church, for leaders, for nations, for families, for marriages etc. I understood that there was to be no set pattern other than to be open to his lead as we met. No one person would own the gathering. God was its author. He would write the script. He would direct it and if there were to be an end, He would end it too. As the day approached that was all I knew. I wondered what everyone would expect of me as I had arranged the meeting and became slightly anxious. I knew no more than what I had told them which, in a nutshell was, "we need to pray." On the morning of the appointed day I asked God, "What shall I do?" and continued to ask throughout the day. As I drove to my mother's home with my daughter, still wondering, I began to feel a strong conviction that on this first meeting we should not pray asking for anything! We were to offer thanksgiving and praise only! We were to take stock of all God had done for us up to that point in our lives, to count our blessings in effect and give thanks, to show our appreciation in abundant praise.

It was a wonderful experience. All of us giving thanks and singing praise and worship together. Remembering times when God showed us His favour. It was a time when my mother recalled how she had asked God for the life of her children and here we all were saved! At this point God revealed that the fervent prayer of a mother had availed much! Now we, her children, were all parents and we began to realise in part why we were called together, one could stand against a thousand, two – ten thousand! Together we were stronger, would achieve more in prayer for our families and who-ever/whatever else we were led to pray for. It became clearer how blessing and curses were passed from one generation to another. Here we were reaping the blessing of a praying mother; and in my nephew and daughter was evidence of it being passed unto a third generation and again in my great nephew, then five months old, the possibility of its continuing onto the fourth generation.

We all left that gathering knowing that it was God's will that we continue to meet monthly and pray together. There was no doubt in anyone's mind at all.

Driving home, I cast my mind back to the day on my knees in my bedroom earnestly asking God for the life of my brothers and sisters, not realising that I had only echoed my mother's prayer, and as with her, God had promised that they would be saved. As I remembered this, I once again saw the building with the top disappearing in the clouds. I saw myself entering the lift, the doors closing and beginning its journey upward. I again sensed I was not alone and turned my head to see who was behind me. Now I'd always known that there were many people in the lift as it travelled up into light, much more than my mere family. I knew this because the tops or sides of their heads were visible. I had seen the odd shoulder or arm and knew there were others in the lift. However, I had not recognised them as they stood behind my family so they had not concerned me. I was only interested in my family and although I did not see the individual faces of my brothers and sisters, I knew or spiritually discerned them all.

As the mini movie of this scene passed before my eyes and I looked on thanking God silently He asked me who I thought the other people were and I said I did not know. I must admit I had wondered over the years but had placed no great importance on them. I looked at them again and wondered why He should ask me! I had never known who they were. They were saved too, that's all I knew! Then, like a light turned on God revealed who they were, they were my family; my nieces and nephews who would come after; my own children. I had not recognised them because they had not existed except in God's plan. They had not been born.
I was astounded! Those I had placed little significance on were my own! I had asked for my generation and He had given another on top and the kernel representing them; one male and one female had been present at the gathering, my nephew and daughter. As I considered that the only one present not saved was my five-month old great nephew, God revealed that he was the promise for his generation!

Isn't that amazing! How great is our God...? And how puny words can appear when you want to express the feelings God evokes within, the wonder, greatness, power and might of God.

I recalled that He had asked, "what could He not do?" if we prayed together and with this revelation of what He had done in response to one prayer I concluded, nothing...Absolutely Nothing.

I had asked for salvation for my family when I was eighteen years old. At forty-four years old God revealed His promise kept, and later at forty six years old, twenty seven years from that vision of the promise, the question I had often asked myself, not really expecting a response, had finally been answered. The others, barely visible were my family! What a revelation!

We have met to pray as a family every month since, and on every occasion we begin by giving thanks and praise to God who has done marvellous things for us. Not including the general things that we wrongly take for granted like waking, breathing etc., we have had many testimonies to share. For me, the highlight was the salvation of my son, and in that, the fulfilment of Gods' promise in 1999. Our family continues to grow so that there are now four generation of believers who have been saved, baptised and filled with the Holy Spirit. We continue to lift those remaining before the Lord in prayer.

He is Able

Over the years and on different continents, I have, as an individual, a wife and a mother, had to face many challenges. I have climbed mountains and waded through deep waters, crossed dry places (metaphorically speaking) and experienced want on a level I did not ever expect to be my portion. Through it all God has been my help, my strength, my hope, my joy, my peace, my rock, and I could continue with a whole assortment of adjectives. Suffice it to say that whatever my need, He supplied it because He is able. Additionally, it was not long before I became aware of hidden depths in me that God through these situations was able to bring to the fore, and strangely enough, while my soul yearned for a simple, smooth, easy life with the 'normal' assortment of ups and downs, I have to admit to a side I was discovering, marvelling at and also finding quite exciting, a side to my character that rose swiftly to a challenge.

The one truth I have grasped and celebrate through all this is the knowledge of the power of praise. I love to praise and worship God in song. I love to sing, but I'm of the opinion that only God can truly appreciate my voice, after all He gave it to me! I'm always singing or humming some tune and out of habit am not always conscious of the fact, until one or other of my children make it clear, they can take no more.

After the break-up of my marriage when I was going through a period of spiritual attack and could barely get through each day, God told me to praise Him and I did. Now you must understand that praising God was the last thing I felt able to do. If He had said curl up under the duvet, feel sorry for yourself and never leave your bed; I could have obeyed easily and willingly. If He had said cry your heart out (what expressions we use!) I could have done that too because I felt as though I could cry forever! But to praise when my distress was like a physical pain that consumed my whole body seemed nigh on impossible. And yet even as I thought it, the realisation that God would not ask me to do what He knew I could not, struck me. I told Him that I did not feel like praising Him. Not that I did not want to, but just that I did not 'feel like it'. And do you know what He said? "What has feelings got to do with it, you praise me because I am God and worthy of your praise!" He was right of course and I obeyed Him. The first few times were the hardest, even to my own ears it was the sorriest sound I had ever heard. I choked on my tears and the words were often lost in my sobs but I praised God because He told me to and because he was worthy of all my praise. I fought to turn my attention from my feelings to His worthiness. I brought to mind His promises and recalled every occasion when He had been there for me. God reminded me daily of the power of praise. He reminded me that He lives in or inhabits praise, which for as long as I praised Him and He dwelled in my praise, there would be no room for Satan who was using my circumstances, my pain to look for a foothold in my life to destroy me. I was reminded of the scripture that speaks of him as a roaring lion seeking whom he may devour (1 Peter 5:8). God revealed Satan's strategy to me and told me that praise was to be my weapon of choice to defeat him. He told me to draw strength from praise, and it was not long before I realised that even though I might begin in response to a command to praise, I was ending with a desire to do so, in fact, at times I found it extremely difficult to stop. I quickly began to recognise certain attacks and before I could sink into self-pity and distress, I would literally burst into song and praise God for who He was and all He had done and would do for me! This was soon followed by the realisation that I should not wait for an attack then defend myself, but should go on the offensive daily with the authority that was mine in Christ. I found myself praising and praying, even when I slept! I first became aware of this one night when I woke to the sound and realised it was coming from me.

I continue to learn of God and in the last several years especially, have been drawn out of my comfort zone and engaged in spiritual warfare on an unprecedented level I did not fully understand existed, and praise has been a major weapon. I have understood that when we praise God, we build a throne for Him and He sits on that throne. When our enemy Satan sees' God on His throne, the throne of our hearts, he is left in no doubt as to who reigns, the same King who defeated him over two thousand years ago. He has no option but to concede defeat yet again. God is able!

The importance of prayer

··•●•··

When God speaks all we can do is align ourselves to his word and wait patiently for its
fulfilment. Of course, being human, we are
prone to forgetfulness and impatience so that
we often cause ourselves a lot of unnecessary
grief. I have come a long way by God's grace.
Where in the past adversity would trigger
worry and disturbed sleep, demonstrating that
I was not walking by faith, now at the first
sign of adversity I cast my thoughts back to
what God had said regarding the situation and
I believe him and live with that knowledge
despite what I see or hear or feel. If he had not
spoken then I'd seek him through prayer and
fasting for guidance. The life of a Christian is
that of a warrior. We have not been misled in
this. If we expect peace and calm, we are de-
luded. Yes, there are periods of peace and
calm, but they should be considered rest periods; like in a game of tennis when each com-
petitor takes time to refresh themselves,
consider their game, develop new strategies,
change their racket, tighten their shoe laces
etc. for the next round. They know there can
be only one winner, so they are prepared to

use every weapon and skill at their disposal. As Christians we have been given all we need to win, in fact the battle is already won in Christ, but we must be in, and remain in him to share the victory, and to do that we must also do battle with our enemy, believing that the victory is ours.

You know, when you seek God, he reveals great mysteries to you. The biggest battle I have fought to date, was that of putting my life and home back together after my husband had left, and for the salvation of our children. At that time, we were the walking wounded and I was the leader. I didn't feel able to lead. I didn't feel strong, and I did not know what to do in that situation. How would I get two hurting and confused children, and myself through each day? How would I help and encourage them when I felt so afraid of the unknown myself? What was the solution to this nightmare?

Mine was a ray of sunshine. Laying in bed on the first morning without my husband my only thought was to pull the duvet over my head, curl up into a tighter ball and stay there forever. I did not feel that I could face the world. I did not think of the children's needs, I only thought of myself and it did not feel good. I wallowed in self-pity for about half an hour and felt even worse. Then the Holy Spirit spoke, "where is God in all of this and what will become of your children if you are not strong for them?" And I thought, "Yeah, where is He?" but I knew the answer, He was where He promised to be, right there with me. He had promised to go through the valley of the shadow of death with me so I was not alone. Knowing this I cried, "Oh no devil, you may have succeeded with my husband but you will not have me or my children". The Holy Spirit's words to me had reminded me that I was a soldier in a battle and the enemy was not my husband who I was very angry with but the spirit behind him. I had wanted to hide under the duvet and shut out the world, but that was not a fighting position, it was one of defeat; so, I prayed, "Lord, help me, give me strength to get out of this bed," and he did. A ray of sunshine broke through a sliver of a gap in the still closed curtains and shone over me. My eyes had been closed but I detected its brightness through my lids and opened them to look up at the window. Some might say it was just normal sunlight, no big deal. I do not doubt that for a moment. But it signified for me the knowledge that God was still on his throne, causing the sun to shine its light. He was still in control, therefore what was I doing behaving as though He had died! I threw the duvet back and leapt out of bed to begin the days' battle.

My prayer life grew massively. I was having two-way conversations like I had never experienced before. It was physically demanding but that was how I got through each day's challenges. I prayed in understanding and in tongues. I fought battles even as I slept and woke to the sound of my voice speaking in tongues. But at times I grew so weary that I would fall asleep in the midst of prayer. This was happening more and more frequently and I thought 'well, you're just tired' so I set myself to sleep more by organising my life differently. No change. I went to my doctor and had a check up and various blood tests looking for an answer. Nothing! I then concluded that it must be age catching up with me even though I was only forty-something. Why not? Our bodies aged differently! I had worked really hard all my life so maybe that was it. What else could it be? I asked God to heal me, assuming I needed healing, the church prayed for me, all with no improvement. Then one night I had a dream.

I dreamt that I was on my knees by my bed praying. I could see myself praying. Then my eyes were raised to look up and as I did, I knew I was looking up into the spirit realm. I saw a mighty warrior in battle dress with shield, breastplate, boots, helmet and sword. Before him, was a large host of smaller, evil looking soldiers with all kinds of weapons advancing and fighting this one big warrior. As far as the eye could see this dark, misshapen host were advancing on the warrior whose armour was golden in colour. As I watched him with his massive sword raised, he made slashing motions from left to right, destroying numerous advancing enemy in one swathe while taking purposeful, sure steps into the advancing host. I then noticed that as the warrior began to take these steps forward, the host began to retreat in confusion, but the warrior did not stop slashing through their ranks and destroying them. My eyes were then drawn down to the image of myself on my knees praying and then back up to the warrior. Recognition came quickly, I was the mighty warrior. God had revealed that every time I prayed in the natural realm, I took on the form of a warrior in the spirit realm and my sword, the word of God, cleaved through my enemies, destroying them, stopping them in their tracks and causing them to flee in all directions.

I was excited by this revelation and understood why I became very tired even at the thought of praying. It had seemed like I had only enough energy to do a day's work. I would get home and fall asleep on the sofa, then be too tired to pray later. Or, when I changed my strategy and went into prayer early before tiredness took over, I would wake up on my knees where I had fallen asleep. I now understood what was happening. My prayers were doing a lot of damage to Satan's kingdom so he was using sleep as his weapon against me. If asleep, I could not pray. Remember when Jesus asked his disciples to pray with him in the garden? They fell asleep. Three times he asked and three times they fell asleep. We all need sleep so or bodies can repair itself, but, if you find all you seem to do is sleep, or when you set yourself to do the Father's will, you are tired, weary, sleepy. If you have excluded health issues and there seems to be no explanation, then consider the enemy. He will do whatever he can to keep you from praying. The Father knows what you need but if you don't ask for it, you won't get it, and, if you don't ask Him what He wants from you, He won't tell you.

However you look at it, prayer is vital, I know, because it has brought me this far.

I talk to God all the time, everywhere, day and night, in sickness and in health, through good and bad times, there is no reason to stop until He calls me or returns. You know, many people commented on how well I seemed to be coping during the separation and divorce and all the challenges this took me through. I'm not perfect by any means, I had weak moments, bad days etc. but the knowledge that God was always there strengthening, encouraging, teaching, comforting, knowing and caring, never left me so that these moments of weakness were short lived. Frequent? Yes, in the early days. Then fewer and further between until, finally, healing took place. And so with this new knowledge I prayed, and listened, and God spoke, and taught me, and instructed me, and brought me through every battle!

Beware, sleep is not the only weapon used against us, it was just his preferred weapon against me. If you were to ask my mother or brothers and sisters what was the one activity, if you can call it that, I never turned down; they would say "sleep". I can't deny that I've made a work of art of it since childhood, so you can see why it was easy to use it against me.

It is not in vain

·· ● ··

You may remember that at one point in my life, reflecting on my role as a wife and mother, my failed marriage and wounded children; that I had ask the question, "Lord, was it all in vain"? He had responded promptly, "No." I had been comforted by this and had waited patiently (mostly) for the salvation of my children. As you can see from my testimony concerning them, salvation came to them both almost one year apart – my daughter in 2003; and my son in 2004. God hears all our prayers as we pray according to His will, but He is Sovereign and answers in His perfect time, not ours, which is often flawed. How many times have you reflected on an answer delayed only to thank God for His perfect timing? Nothing that we do for Him, if living in obedience is in vain, as a mother who believes that children are a gift from God, who believes that God required me to train them up in the knowledge of Him by word, by deed, and by example. I determined to be a good wife and mother. The Holy Spirit was my guide. I talked to him all the time and positively ran to him when faced with any situation that called for prompt, decisive, sustainable action.

My encouragement to you is to hold on to the Lord, to what is good. Bring all your petitions before him and pray them through. That is why we have been commanded to pray without ceasing and in everything give thanks. When we trust and serve the Lord, on His terms not our own, nothing we do will ever be in vain as God's purposes for our lives are fulfilled.

Printed in Great Britain
by Amazon

86310705R00139